SOARING

*Mounting Up as Eagles
in the Midst of Turmoil*

RITA COMER

SOARING: Mounting Up as Eagles in the Midst of Turmoil

Published by:
RMC Ministries
rmc_ministries@yahoo.com

Book Creation and Design
DHBonner Virtual Solutions, LLC
www.dhbonner.net

ISBN: 978-0-578-72679-3

Printed in the United States of America

This book is dedicated to my grandchildren:
Mercy Grace, Liberty Joy, Joah Joshua, Prudence Faith, and Kohen Elijah. I pray you and your future seed never encounter the mistakes, the trials, and pain
of all your previous generations.

"Trust in the Lord with all your heart, and lean not on your own understanding; In all your ways acknowledge Him, and He shall direct your paths."
-Proverbs 3:5-6

I pray that the Word of God will always lead you
on the paths He has planned for you. May you experience God's victory as you develop your skills in becoming effective, fervent warriors in His kingdom! As warriors
of God, may you always have the tenacity
to overcome your enemies in prayer!

I DECREE and DECLARE
that God's favor and the blood of Jesus Christ
will always cover you as you excel into
the purposes and plans of God.

Table of Contents

Foreword

I invite you to come into the personal world of a gifted writer. She tells it all in order to give insight into practical and Spiritual applications, which will catapult you into higher dimensions of life as you enter into self-discovery.

As you read this book, you will become engulfed in several stages of your own life as she so intimately shares her experiences. Some writers superficially touch your life; however, this book will penetrate to the core and expose areas you may have chosen not to deal with — but must to become complete and whole.

You will notice how she uses Scriptures as life rafts to carry you safely through the storm of life and bring you safely to shore. She uses the Word of God to bring you to shore and then goes further to show you how to travel the back roads, side streets, alleyways, roundabouts, highways, and bi-ways you will encounter once you find land.

Each chapter is power-packed and filled with tried and proven golden nuggets to lead you through the difficulties of your past, the troubles of your present, and the realness of your future. Rita not only brings hope, but also an excitement of what awaits for those who choose to employ the methodologies inserted in each segment of the game-changing book, and she uses personal family experiences to bring clarity to some of the questions you may have had concerning your childhood.

She does not leave any stone unturned! Then, she uses the role of the Holy Spirit in your life, which will lead and guide you. She uses how difficult that can be, especially when you have to leave a place and move to another. Being led by the Spirit and obeying what is being said is not easy when it goes against every fiber of desire within you. However, again she uses her personal battles to lead you to personal victories.

You will not want to put this book aside because it covers such a wide spectrum of life's vicissitudes. She incorporates sensitive and complex subjects that include blended families and shattered covenants. These are areas that are so common and are on a seemingly slippery slope with very little success of recovery. This author addresses these concerns head-on with no reservations and provides options that, when applied with prayer, faith, and aggression, will undoubtedly make an indelible difference in the trajectory of your focus towards success.

The author uses her walk of life as a paintbrush — each encounter a stroke on the canvas that draws a road map of how to navigate through your life and successfully arrive at your destination of purpose and meaningful contributions — to advance your life and the kingdom of God.

Lastly, you will benefit from using the journal at the end of this book. Use it as a daily "Fitbit" to monitor and control your daily growth and progress. This is an all-inclusive system (not just a book) that will heighten your daily walk with God and expand your overall quality of life. . . in all areas.

Bishop Norman Hardman
Mount of Transfiguration Church
Opelika, AL

With Special Thanks

To my husband, Milton Comer, God showed me you in my dream, years before we ever met. Your face was not clear, but He assured me that, one day, I would marry this person. My walk down the aisle was truly one of my happiest days. Although we didn't expect some things that happened, I'm glad you came into my life. The love I have for you taught me true forgiveness.

Certain parts of this book could not have been written without you. God has a way of showing us how "all things do work together for the good to those who love Him." He works the good, bad, and ugly for His good and allows the love to remain. I pray God's purpose will be fulfilled, in new ways, as He shifts you to higher levels in Him. I thank you, and I will always love you.

***

To my loving daughter and son-in-love, Lashonda and Mark Coles, you make a mother proud. There were many things you did behind the scenes. Thank you for blessing me with my beautiful grandchildren. Mark, you are indeed an answer to the many prayers I prayed over Lashonda, as she grew up to become the mighty woman of God that she is today. It was because of her that I learned to get really specific with my prayer strategies. I'm so blessed to have witnessed many of them, answered with you. God's hand and favor are upon you both. Thank you for always showing love. I love you both to life!

***

To Joann Alcox, our friendship goes back for over forty plus years. As your new nineteen-year-old employee, you became my first supervisor in my IT (Internet Technology) career. It didn't take long to realize we would become special friends, and you would impact me and my daughter's life.

You saw me grow up before your eyes, but I saw the love you showed to many on the job. You pushed us to excel into purpose, and you still have pushed me over the years, saying, "Pray and trust God. Don't give up. God has you, and I'm here for you." This was so very true for you were there just in the nick of time. Thank you for expressing your love in so many ways and being a friend who always speaks life in the power of your tongue. Love you!

***

To Valarie Harvey, my prayer warrior, my 'iron sharpening iron' buddy. Words cannot express what's in my heart. Thank you for always telling me what I "need" to hear in love and not just what I "want" to hear. I married into the family, but you always made me feel like family throughout our friendship. I will be forever grateful. Thanks for really praying me through some difficult places, as far back as Indiana. You let me cry through some of the worst storms. When life crushed me, you prayed the broken pieces back together. You spoke words of life when I wanted to give up on life, and for this, I'll always love you!

***

And last, but not least . . . *to my mom, Erma Roper*, a praying woman who prayed me out of the prison of my soul and into ministry! She knew this book was in the making before her death and supported me in continuing — to tell the truth. She encouraged me to stay with God when I couldn't see past the storms in life. She reminded me that just because you don't see what you are praying for, doesn't mean God won't bring the answer in His own time.

I thank God that He planted me in her womb; I will forever carry her love within my heart. Mom was my biggest supporter in life. I believe she's still a big supporter, even in death, as a part of that great cloud of witnesses. It encourages me to lay aside every weight and run with endurance the race set before me. Thank you for helping me to go forward to complete this book! I go forward with God leading me!

So, rest on, Mom. Your love will continue to flow through me, and I will always love you!

Introduction

This book is written for those who encounter paths of persecutions, trials, and turmoil in many areas of their life, thinking their life has no purpose, meaning, or value. You are valuable in the kingdom of God — regardless of what has taken place in your life, God has made you able to soar above life's turmoil and hold on to your faith, no matter how severe the storm. The trials we face can remind me of eagles facing a coming storm. While we may find a safe place to take cover, hiding from the weather elements, I learned that eagles love the storms. They are not afraid of them, no matter how fierce or powerful the wind may be. With spread wings, the eagles use the wind to lift them effortlessly toward the sky, soaring above the storms.

So, it can be that way with us when we are facing turmoil in life. Either we can run and hide, letting the storms overwhelm us — which include hurricanes and tornadoes — or we can allow it to take us to a greater height in the Lord to develop our Christian character.

Life happens. There may be certain things we would have done differently if given a chance. When we look back, in retrospect, and see the alternative paths that God wanted us to take, we learn wisdom from our past experiences, mistakes, or hurts. Even when the path causes much pain, stay strong in your faith and determine in your heart not to let the painful paths of turmoil separate you from the love of Christ Jesus.

Perhaps you lost your identity to someone you gave too much control or power over your life; power, you discover almost too late, should have never been taken out of God's hand. Maybe you live a lifestyle of un-holiness, and redirection from God led you into holiness. What about father or mother issues? It could be that you miss out on a father's love, making it hard for you to relate to God the Father. What about the heart of a loving mother that you would discover after a much-strained relationship? Maybe, it wasn't all bad for you, because you received an unexpected blessing from unexpected places or people. Perhaps you were very comfortable in life, and here comes the Lord, telling you to MOVE from something or someplace! It might be that you're a part of a blended family, but discover you are not blending very well with them, nor are they with you.

Maybe you experience a troubled marriage, due to both parties not walking in total healing, or truthfulness. Maybe covenant relationships were broken, leaving you in a broken state that would need the power of God to repair your brokenness. Perhaps you experienced so many deep losses in life that it seems like it's hard to continue believing in the things of God. Maybe you lose your ability to dream again, due to many disappointments in life.

If you experience any of the above, you are not by yourself; I'm right there with you. "For we know that all things work together for good to those who love God, to those who are the called according to *His* purpose." This Scripture is not saying everything terrible that happens to us is good, but that it is working together for our good. What path is God getting ready to take you on to fulfill destiny or His purpose for you? Everything you went through was preparing you for destiny. Whatever route you had to take, let His process lead you to completion, so that God can get the glory.

Life can take us on some paths of turmoil that we may have never seen coming. What we learn from God's wisdom can help someone else in their life. They will either learn what to do or what not to do. My story shows how our messes in life can become messages that God can use to teach others. Some people put others in bondage because they are afraid of the truth to be told. It's the truth that makes us free when we choose to face the truth about ourselves, instead of the enemy's lies. Isn't that what John 8:32 is about? It reads, "And you shall know the truth, and the truth shall make you free."

Writing this book reveals my vulnerabilities, weaknesses, failures, bad decisions, and thoughts during rough times. You may have encountered much of the same, having trials that made you want to quit in life. Trust the process God sometimes allows through many difficult trials, challenges, and situations. His way is perfect. His Word is perfect. He makes no mistakes. You may have veered off His paths, but He has a perfect way of redirecting you back onto the right track. Trust Him and lean not unto your own understanding. He'll lead you back onto the path toward His will.

Why? Because you have a story to tell also, and no one can tell your story better than you! This book will impact your life to move forward, soaring above whatever turmoil that has tried to keep you from succeeding in Christ. Personal and biblical stories, along with biblical principles and applications, will be shared to show how God can use any situation or person in turmoil to triumph in life. No matter what has happened, don't let it persuade you from the love of God. Let Him speak and lead you into victory over adverse situations.

Don't let the trials consume you. You can expect to experience a breakthrough and healing, by believing that what God did for someone else, He is determined to do for you!

> Then the Lord answered me and said: "Write the vision and make *it* plain on tablets, that he may run who reads it." -Habakkuk 2:2

Lost Identity

What do you do when the challenges of life throw you a curveball, leaving you so emotionally bruised, with a severe blow to your self-esteem or identity? What do you do when it seems like your identity has been hijacked or stolen by the enemy? You may find yourself coming out of those challenges, not knowing who you really are. All you want to do is withdraw and hide from the stares and comments of critical eyes. That's what losing your identity seems like.

Life can take you on a roller coaster ride that includes many ups, downs, twists, turns, loops, thrills, and fears. Depending on what part of that roller coaster ride you're on, it may leave you feeling that it was the best or worst ride of your life. On the scariest part of that ride, it may be hard to fake a smile when your life seems to have been ripped apart. It may even be hard to keep the faith when it seems like God is breaking you into a million pieces. Isn't one broken piece enough? Do you really have to be broken into a million pieces?

That roller coaster ride may include . . . depression and suicidal thoughts, stolen peace, troubled relationships, or many other life losses. When a ride has been bad, you're just glad to get off. That's what losing your identity seems like. But you can recover from a lost identity, just like you can recover from a bad ride.

Many things contribute to my lost identity: Experiencing rejection, fears, childhood and adult traumas, false responsibilities, growing up in alcoholic environments, bad relationships, abuse, and betrayal. I didn't know who I was, and I surely didn't know who I was in Christ. It was years before I discovered that identity in Christ.

The loss of my identity could not be dealt with until I realized that I genuinely had a problem. The problem could not be dealt with until I admitted my problem with depression and the things that led up to it. If the enemy had his way, I would not be sharing my story now. I would be in some cemetery, six feet under, never to impact a life, or fulfill a purpose. It was a loss that included much depression with suicidal thoughts. The thoughts lead me to want to end my life. The only part of Psalm 42:5 (NIV) I could reflect on was the question, "Why, my soul, are you downcast? Why so disturbed within me?" For many years I could never get into my heart the part that read, "Put your hope in God, for I will still praise Him, my Savior and my God."

With the first attempt, I had no Word in my spirit to sustain me. I was a "churchgoer only" who didn't apply God's principles! I had no real, intimate relationship with the Father! I took notes in church, but didn't go back to review them! I heard preachers preach, yet forgot their message as soon as I left the building during those early years. When anyone asked me what the pastor preached on, I could not give them a summary. I would just say that I didn't know, but it sure was good, and they should have been there! Perhaps they should have been there because I was not a good witness to others.

I was a carnal Christian, conformed to this world with no identity, and depression had a hold of me! I was a single mother, working full-time, going to college full-time, raising my daughter, and overwhelmed by the pressures of life. It seemed like my whole life had been one troubling event after another; I was at a point where I just gave up trying. I was always in a position of taking care of everyone else, from the time I was a child, but where were those who were supposed to take care of me? It would be many years later before I learned about the false responsibilities I carried that should have been carried by adults only.

The day I decided to end my life, I definitely was not thinking clearly. When everything darkened within from the dose of pills I had taken, God spoke clearly to my inner man. At that time, I didn't know anything about hearing the voice of God, the Prophetic, or that there was a call on my life in that area. God said something that stayed with me, "Rita, if you would just change your ATTITUDE, I'll change your ALTITUDE!" In my mind, I was saying, "How do I do that, Lord?"

See, there was a battlefield taking place in my mind, from years of bad thinking and not knowing who I was in Christ! What the Lord was telling me to do was change the way I was thinking. Wrong thinking led me to have suicidal thoughts. He wanted me to switch to His way of thinking to change the circumstances in my life! My lifestyle changed when I began to apply God's Word and principles into my life.

Starting on my road toward healing, I had to fast from negative thinking, replacing the enemy lies with God's truth; I "was transformed by the renewing of my mind." Then, I was able to prove what was the "good, acceptable, and perfect will of God" for my life. I also had to withdraw from some toxic, unhealthy people, until I was able to gain strength from God to break free from bondage.

As my attitude changed, God did change my altitude! This change manifested strongly in my corporate career, taking me from my hometown of Gary, Indiana to the Pittsburgh, Pennsylvania region to the Atlanta, Georgia area and all of the way to a small city called Opelika, Alabama! But depression and the suicidal thoughts followed me to each of those cities; you'll read about those stories in a later chapter.

The enemy may try to bring hindrances, like lost identity, depression, and suicidal thoughts, to stop us from reaching destiny! But, when God has souls assigned to our hands, it does not matter if we have to press past every hindrance toward healing, deliverance, and counseling, and then taking whatever form of transportation to reach those souls. He will get us there if we allow Him!

The change God did, allowed me to walk out deliverance in many areas! But how many of you know that, just like the devil left Jesus in the wilderness for a more opportune and favorable time, he seeks that same opportunity to steal, kill and destroy us, when it's more advantageous for his plans of destruction in our life! For a while, the enemy did nothing to prompt me in that area, as I grew in God's Word, applying His principles. In this chapter, I won't go into every detail about the things that lead to depression and suicidal thoughts. Still, they included, over the years, a combination of much turmoil, trauma, rejection, betrayal on many levels, and physical, verbal, and emotional abuse. After a significant betrayal took place, the depression and suicidal thoughts returned with an overwhelming vengeance. The devil also came back for what he thought was "his more opportune time for destruction," prompting me with another attempt to take my life!

This time, he was clear that because the pills didn't work last time, it would be quicker to take that 357 Magnum in my hands and blow my brains out. I believed the enemy's lie, that no one cared about me in the place I was living. After all, it was the place where I experienced my greatest hurt. The enemy overplayed his hand and did not count on God's stepping in with divine intervention. I'll always be thankful for the person He sent, just in time, before the trigger was pulled. I can honestly say, as King David said in the Psalm to the Lord, "For You have delivered my soul from death."

God can save us from the enemy, even when he has lied to get into our soul. After this, I was forced to deal with everything that had caused me to walk away from my identity. Thank God for growth in His Word, His power, His strength, His healing, His protection, His intervention, and His deliverance! Now, I'm able to sense that suicidal spirit around others who have it. When counseling is not working with that individual, I intervene in prayer, on their behalf, to the Lord and have seen lives changed. Jesus came that we might have life and to have it more abundantly! I chose life and the will to live, like so many others! After walking away from depression and suicide, God moved to restore my lost identity. When God delivers you from places of brokenness, like you're reading in this book, you can become a vessel that He can use to help deliver others.

Not knowing who you are in Christ is not a good place to be, but God never lets us go when we're holding on to His promises. Thank God for the power of His Word and His Presence to sustain us. As I became aware of His help to me, I also became aware of being used for His purpose. God continued to strengthen and hardened me through all kinds of difficulties. He continued to hold me up and retain me with His right hand of righteousness and justice, even when I didn't want to hold on to Him.

We have many Scriptures from the New Testament that we can meditate on to tell us who we are in Christ. Sometimes, I read the Old Testament to learn about biblical characters who may have suffered similar things. As I walked out my newly-found identity, I discovered that Jacob, Moses, and Saul appear to have suffered from some type of identity crisis. As I read about these characters, I related more to Moses.

Moses was born to Hebrew parents, yet raised by Pharaoh's daughter as an Egyptian. Acts 7:22, states that he "was learned in all the wisdom of the Egyptians, and was mighty in words and deeds." But Moses also knew about his background, and when he was grown, he killed an Egyptian for oppressing one of his brethren, a Hebrew slave. Moses may have felt he just didn't fit in with the Egyptians because they were oppressing his people. Neither did he fit in with the Hebrews, because he wasn't treated like them as slaves.

There have been times and places that I also just didn't fit in. God never designed Moses or me to fit into anybody's plan, but His! Certain environments caused me to feel suffocated when they were trying to mold me into what they thought I should be. For years, I allowed others to mold me, just like Moses was molded into the Egyptians' culture. Moses fled for his life and stayed away for many years until "the Angel of the Lord appeared to him in a flame of fire from the midst of a bush." It was time for Moses to go on his assignment to deliver his people from Egypt. Wait . . . What? I, too, tried to flee, but it was in the wrong way; the enemy wanted my life.

Moses didn't know who he was, but he had a call on his life, like many of us. Moses had an identity crisis when he asked God in Exodus 3:11, "Who *am* I that I should go to Pharaoh and bring the children of Israel out of Egypt?" If that was not enough, he then gave God several excuses and asked God, "O my Lord, please send by the hand of whomever *else* You may send." Moses was no more confident than I was swallowing those pills when I wanted to take my life. The call of God was on my life then, just as much as it is now, but I just didn't know it. We both had the backing of God.

The enemy hijacked our identity, and it blinded us to who we were with God until we stepped into purpose. Moses went on to deliver his people out of bondage. It's funny that my life, as you will read, will also be led out of much bondage, with deliverance taking place in many areas. As the Lord has delivered me, He has also used me to help deliver others as I gain my newfound identity in Christ.

You may be in a place where you are crying out to the Lord, asking Him, "Who am I, Lord? I don't really know right now! What is it that you want me to do? My little life doesn't matter." That's not what God thinks; John 3:16 reads, "For God so loved the world that He gave His only begotten Son, that whoever believes in Him should not perish but have everlasting life." God does not want you to perish, no more than He wanted me to. He didn't give us His only begotten Son so that we can live a life of not knowing who we are in Christ. Your life is not meaningless or purposeless in His eyes.

You are alive right now with Christ. The Spirit of God, who is greater than the enemy in the world, lives within you. Christ has given you authority and power over the enemy in this world! You have the power of the Holy Spirit living within you, and He can do miraculous things through you. How? Why? Because you have the Mind of Christ! Your new identity is found in Christ. Whatever He needs you to do, trust Him! If your need in life aligns with His will, you have nothing to fear. You can do whatever you need to do in life through Christ Jesus, who gives you strength! You were chosen for such a time as this! You were chosen by God, forgiven, and justified through Christ. Christ lives in you, and you live by faith in Him.

This is a new day to press on and fulfill God's plan for your life because you live to please Him. Walk in your identity, which is found in Christ Jesus!

Un-holiness to Holiness

> "But as He who called you *is* holy, you also be holy in all *your* conduct, because it is written, "Be holy, for I am holy." -1 Peter 1:15-16

O*ur past helped shape* our future, even when God moves us from un-holiness to a lifestyle of holy living. Many have walked away from a sinful past that, if it were not for God's grace, we would still be deep in sin. If we never share how God brought us out of our messes, how would we ever be able to help somebody else get out of theirs?

Although I grew up attending church, I didn't always display God's principles living in me. I couldn't because I didn't have an intimate relationship with the Lord, and I didn't serve Him faithfully as my Lord and Savior. I modeled what I saw growing up, and it was far from holy living.

In most of the churches I attended, sin was not addressed much, and I didn't see lives transformed. As a teenager, I only went to church on Sundays, so that I could attend the weekly movies and teen dances. If I didn't go to church, I could not go to my weekly outings. So, my cousins and I went, watching and mocking the people in the church who were jumping up all over the place. During the week, we would see some of these same people drinking, getting high on dope, and partying up a storm. Then we saw the married ones going out with boyfriends or girlfriends (indicating unfaithfulness to their spouses), we could only imagine where to.

Before I was a teenager, I would always visit and stay at a particular family member's house. The landlord's house was in front, with a basement, and I used to call it the "House of Sin". Although I was young, I knew what went on in that basement. I went down there often with the landlord, to see her clean the rooms and wash the sheets. I said, "Oh, this is nothing but a hotel in a basement."

There was a key on a big ring, kept at the back house, and people would always knock on the door when the landlord was not home. As a little girl, I opened the door, and they would ask, "Do you have the key to the basement?" I asked them, "Do you have the money?" Then I would tell them the cost. I was instructed to never give out the key unless I got the money first. Then I told them to bring that key back before they walked down the stairs; I might need to give it to somebody else to get in. I watched them unlock the door, and then return the key to me. I was a child surrounded amid un-holy living. You can't see all that un-holiness of sin in life and not be affected by it.

Proverb 22:6 says, "Train up a child in the way he should go, and when he is old he will not depart from it." Sadly, I was trained to head toward a lifestyle of un-holiness before I would walk in holiness with Christ. I'm sure this was not the way God originally planned for us to be trained. I saw and experienced things a child should never experience.

Where I grew up, the adults loved to party, drink, and have fun. There were times that the children were left with those they trusted to babysit. They should never have trusted some, nor left developing girls with men, or boys, who had no control over their sexual urges. We hear about sexual abuse or molestation among children on the news today, but it was also going on when I was young. It was just hushed, not talked about a lot. It can rob a child of their innocence and purity in life. It causes them not to look at people the same. It makes it hard to trust those that are supposed to protect you. It reveals entry points to the enemy who can come in, affecting attitudes and the child's outlook on life.

Your mind can be invaded by oppression and depression, all because you were among those with un-holy lifestyles. The enemy loves to steal, kill, and destroy our destiny as children, so we will not fulfill God's call on our life. The enemy overplayed his hand with me because God definitely took me toward purpose.

Life has taken me through many ups, downs, and turbulent years into un-holiness. My Mom used to say, "Sin is pleasurable for a season, but it comes at a cost." During those times, I didn't know what the cost was until 1987 when the Lord began to pull me into His kingdom. I thought, 'Ok, Lord, I'll give my life to you, but I don't want to date those you have in the church.' I was just like some other sisters going to church. We didn't see anyone in there worth having. As singles, we saw men who did not know how to treat their wives and dated us — if we gave them a chance. We saw men who were not living holy, but were churchgoers, looking for the next woman to conquer.

I struggled when God said, "Let the men go that you are dating." I was like . . . no way, no one was in church that impressed me. The enemy knows what we like, how to dress them, and brings them to us, entrapping us in ungodly lifestyles. There was a time when he brought a man into the church with the goal of leading me away from purpose. I didn't know that I was in the midst of purging and preparation for my call.

God also sent a young lady who was instrumental in helping me walk toward holiness; several people would ask me if I had met her yet. When we met, I don't think we liked each other at first, because we may have prejudged one another. While at a lay meeting with the pastor, she had started up a fruitful single ministry and asked if I wanted to help her. I rolled my eyes, which told her, "No, I'm not ready to live holy or righteous as a single." We became best friends over time. Years later, she introduced me to her cousin, who became my husband. I didn't know that she flowed (she was in and spoke) prophetically and saw my life change as God began to shape and grow me toward my prophetic purpose.

He started by causing relationships to end; He told me the reason why. God said:

> I told you to end it, and since you didn't listen, it will be a while before you get into a relationship with another man. There's too much that I want to do through you; the cost of where you are going to walk is high. To whom much is given, much is required. Much is required for you to walk in holiness because of the call on your life. Only those that are a part of your destiny will be able to come along.

I was like, "What cost? What call? What have You called me to do?" I didn't learn the answer for many years. Revelation 3:7 says, "And to the angel of the church in Philadelphia write, 'These things says He who is holy, He who is true,' "He who has the key of David, He who opens and no one shuts, and shuts and no one opens."

When God blocks, no one can remove the blocks. When He closes doors, no one can open them until He is ready for them to be opened. He meant what He said. It was eight long years before He opened the door to a relationship. God moved me from Indiana to Pennsylvania to continue applying many biblical principles, which helped me live a successfully single life with a lifestyle of holiness. He moved me to

Georgia, where deliverance took place, removing stuff that took place during those childhood years of un-holiness.

My cousin confirmed, with prophecy, what God spoke into my life in Indiana. He said, "I see you sitting in a chair just as happy and smiling. God's favor is upon you. It's your time. To whom much is given, from him much will be required. Get ready for what God wants to do through you." It was years before I saw myself as someone valuable that God could use.

Walking in holiness does not mean that you won't experience any hurts — just ask Hosea. According to different versions and translations of the Bible, when the Lord spoke to Hosea, He told him to marry a prostitute, a wife of whoredom, a wife of harlotry, an unfaithful woman, a woman who has sex with anyone, a wife of fornications. In other words, marry a whore! This was obviously a marriage full of pain and trouble because Gomer did not walk in holiness at all.

We are not guaranteed a life free of pain and trouble because we walk in holiness. Even in righteousness, I had my share of redirection from the Lord. When I met my husband, God reminded me of what He had told me years earlier. He told me to keep the relationship holy; do not cross the line sexually, or this relationship would end, too.

By this time, I had too much reverent fear of the Lord to miss out on His blessings. I had learned by experience that He meant what He said and would close doors if I stepped over the line sexually. Although I was fighting the call on my life for years, I began to embrace that God was indeed calling me to do something in the ministry. I didn't know what, but I recognized that it would cause me to walk at a higher level.

When it was evident that the relationship would lead to marriage, we spent as much time as we could together. I can remember my pastor telling me to keep the relationship holy. He stated that most people let their guards down when they know they are closer to marriage; that's when they start having sex. The Holy Spirit put a check within my spirit while dating. This led me to 1 Thessalonians 5:22, which reads, "Abstain from every form of evil." I knew, instantly, where the Lord was going.

We lived in two different states. When I first came to visit him, I stayed in a hotel. Later, I stayed at his place and vice versa. Responding to the Lord's rebuke, I said, 'I haven't sinned with this man, and I am not fornicating with him; I'm living holy.' There's no reasoning with God when there is a call on your life. God spoke to my spirit, saying, "The point is that you didn't shun the appearance of sin. So, most people will not think that if you stay over at his place and he stays over at yours. There's a call on your life, and the cost is high!" I did not learn the cost of the call, until after I got married.

I thought that by walking in holiness, I would be spared pain. Just like Hosea, pain entered in. I had to learn to be faithful, even when people are not faithful to me. I had to forgive, no matter how hard it was, for my benefit. I had to release the anger that I had toward God. I asked Him what purpose He had for my walking through this type of pain. What was the purpose of walking in holiness? I didn't want what Hosea had. God let me cry and scream until I stopped. He spoke when I calmed down. He said:

> Look over your prophecies, and let me tell you the purpose. I've called you to deliver many people. How can you deliver others if you have never been in captivity to anything? I called you to war on behalf of the people that I put around you! You are a warrior in MY KINGDOM! You're going to see My people get set free! I have called you to do what I show you to do! You're going to lead MY PEOPLE and set the captive free!

There's an anointing on your life that I placed there! I'll break off anything and anybody that will hold you back! Because of the freedom I put within you, you're going to begin to impart some things to other people around you! I'm going to start to open up the doors for you! My purpose and My plan are greater!

There are hearts that I want you to reach! You are going to bring, not only deliverance, but also healing to many! I will block any attack from the enemy that comes against you, no matter who it is! You just stay focused!

I have not called you to go through this life with weights and burdens to hold you back! I called you to move forward in Me! Every trial and everything the enemy tried to bring, I brought you through like a shining star!

I'm going to anoint your hand to write and use the creativity I've put within you! Don't you fear! You've been through the storms that I allowed to come your way, and you've been able to weather them! I'm acting upon your Word!

I have the plan, and I have the purpose! You went through the storms for a particular reason, so that you would be able to minister to others, as I brought you through! Your prayers are heard, and you will see answers!

Someone reading this needed to hear words of encouragement from the Lord. Perhaps, in your un-holy living, there was turmoil due to the neglect or mistakes of others. God was with you way back then. He never forsakes you, nor does He leave you. There may have been many things He protected you from that you didn't see or know about.

His purpose and plan for you are far greater than yours. He desires you to walk in holiness so that you can have an intimate relationship with Him. He desires to speak to you and lead you away from the turmoil that ungodliness has brought your way. Even when others are not faithful to you, God will always be faithful to you. No, you might not have been spared pain, but God will strengthen you so that you can fulfill and walk in His purpose!

A Father's Love

"When my father and my mother forsake me, then the Lord will take care of me." -Psalm 27:10

T*he above Scripture always* makes me realize that the Lord started taking care of me at an early age. I hadn't even started school when my parents divorced. Although both parents were living, I felt forsaken by my father, even back then. I don't know enough of his history or background to understand his struggles.

It was not a long marriage. Mom was sixteen, and my father was eighteen when they had me; I don't have too many memories of them together. I can remember visiting him in Chicago after the divorce; he lived with someone else. I don't know how he ended up with me, but it was quite a surprise to the woman he was living with. She was definitely letting him know she was not going to take care of that woman's child, although I'm putting it in a nice way. I remember her throwing his clothes out the window and cussing him out because I was there. He just sat there with a hung head. I cried for my Mom because I didn't want to be there. Mom must have come for me, because I didn't see him much after that.

I grew up wanting the love of a father, but never got that from him in the way I needed it. I never knew what was going on with him. I'm sure he had his own set of issues that no one helped him with. If it wasn't for his sister, one of my favorite aunts, I don't believe I would have had much connection with that side of my family. This aunt made it possible for me to see him over the years, but it was mostly in mental hospitals. I was young and asked her, "If he is crazy, I don't want to go to the hospital to see him like that. How come we don't see him when he's out?" She said, "Rita, that is your father." I told her that I didn't know him, and I didn't want to go.

I had started to develop a bad attitude toward my father. I felt that if he really wanted to be around, he would. I felt hurt, neglected, rejected, and even betrayed by his lack of love toward us. I didn't know this would affect me in my later years with others, or as a Christian. My heart was hardened; I played into the enemy's lie that I didn't need him. Over the years, I got used to his absences for anything important like . . . visits, money, school activities, birthdays, holidays, graduation, and even for my wedding.

There were other siblings that we didn't see much growing up. I didn't develop a relationship with one brother until we were around thirteen years old — when my aunt took me to meet him. My father had gotten both of our mothers pregnant around the same time, with only a five-month difference. I am the oldest of his children.

Because he never made much effort to see me, I believed the lies of the enemy: "You are not worth his time. He has more important things to do instead of seeing you." As a child, when I discovered that his attention was given more to the other siblings, it added fuel to the fire, causing me to think, "Why can't he just love us all the same?"

The hurts and wounds of a father's rejection lay dormant within me for years. I felt, not only rejected, but betrayed because he was supposed to be there, or so I thought. We were supposed to be close. I remembered this again, later in life, when betrayal returned by someone else who was supposed to be close. This thinking caused me to have a distorted and wrong viewpoint of my Heavenly Father when I accepted Christ. It wasn't until my adult life that I discovered he loved me the best way he could. I also had to deal with the feelings of not being valued by him or others. As a prophet, I discovered later that it's not unusual for hurt and betrayal to follow a prophet's life.

During my senior year, my aunt took me to see my father in the hospital. She had done that over the years since that was the only way I was going to see him. Those visits were always traumatic for me because of the craziness I observed among the patients.

On this visit, I had to enter the ward by myself. I wasn't expecting the security guard to lock me in. I walked past a glass window where workers were gathered. A doctor with a stethoscope around his neck met me and asked who I was looking for. When I told him the name, he said his room was over to my left. He went to the door, peeked in, and said he must be in the lounge.

He led me to the packed lounge; all heads turned to watch me. My father was drugged, but he knew who I was. He asked me how I knew he was in the lounge. The doctor had sat down to watch me also, so I told my father that the doctor told me. He slightly rolled his eyes and said he wasn't a doctor, but a patient like him. The doctor-patient smiled at me, yet continues to watch me. He watched me so much that it bothered my dad. When he asked my dad for a cigarette looking at me, my dad jumped up, yelling at him that I was his daughter! Doctor-patient walked away. I was ready to go, but that was the only time I remember my father being protective of me.

All of a sudden, an older lady who looked to be in her eighties started cussing me out. She told me I was too young to be messing with that man, my father. She said, "Witch, I should kick your butt," although these were not her exact words. I was in shock, but the only thing my drugged father could say was, "Sometimes you think they're talking to you, sometimes they're not." I saw her talking to and coming for me, cussing ups a storm. The doctor-patient jumped up, saying he couldn't take this or her anymore.

A commotion started, and the real workers had to come to calm them down. I was on the verge of tears, but my father couldn't help me because he was in need. The old lady cussed me out, even when they escorted her out of the lounge. The only thing my father could say over and over was the previous statement.

It was years later that I discovered God was with me when I walked into that place. To calm the people down, Mr. DJ-patient put on the Drifters' song, "Under the Boardwalk." One by one, each of those patients joined in to sing that song. My father and I were the only ones, not singing. I felt surrounded by craziness and crazy people! Every time I hear that song, I think of that visit, and the statement my father kept repeating over and over. I hated that song initially, but now it brings a smile to my face.

I wanted to run out crying; however, I didn't do it then. My father hugged me and walked me part of the way, until the old lady returned to cuss me out again. She told me she was ready to kick my butt for messing with that old man. By then, I lost it and was trying to escape through the locked door.

The security guard let me out; however, he would not let me leave until I calmed down. He wanted to make sure that I was ok before I left. He said they were watching while I was there and wouldn't have let any harm come to me. I knew that was the last time that I would see him in a place like that, ever again.

Amazingly, some turmoil we go through can leave us feeling like we are all by ourselves. But God has His eyes on us the whole time. I didn't know then that I was under the protection of my heavenly Father. When people talked about God being our Father, I based this on my experience with my natural father — which were not always good for me — or on what I saw with others. When I gave my life to the Lord, I had to give him all of the hurt, hatred, disappointments, and frustration of missing out on being a "Daddy's girl." I had to learn that, just because I had a lousy representation on earth, God was nothing like my father. There were many feelings to deal with before my father went home to the Lord. That senior year, I received my first present from him for graduation; I did not see another one until I was married.

I never had "the talk" with a fatherly figure to know what to look for in men, and along the way, I made some bad choices. Not all of the men were bad, but there were a couple who had narcissistic behavior. There were some that I should never have trusted and really could have used the godly wisdom of a father who was in a right relationship with the Lord.

When I moved away from Gary, I talked to him more than I did while growing up. When I visited him, I could see the joy and love — that he was delighted to see me. At his funeral, the stories people told about the way he talked about me, really encouraged me. I never knew he loved or cared about me like that. At the cemetery, when everyone was getting into the cars, I was still hugging people. It was just my cousin and me; as she hugged me, the tears flowed . . . for all I had missed in my relationship with him. But I was glad to know that I always had my father's love.

I may have felt forsaken by my father, but God did provide a fatherly figure with my mother's father. This is who I called Daddy. He was no Granddad or Grandpa; he was Daddy. He was there for a lot of what was important in my life. I'll always have special memories of him. When Mom pulled a drunken episode, or we were at war, Daddy was who I called. I might not have known about being my father's girl, but I was definitely my grandfather's girl.

I do believe many of his grandkids felt that way because he thought his grandchildren could do anything. We all did have our successes in many activities. We saw him at parades we were in. Daddy was proud of us all. His love produced honor students, beauty queens, ministers, prophets, doctors, nurses, star hall of fame basketball, and other sports players. He would be proud of how many of us took off in our careers and businesses. He didn't live to see me develop my career, but he would be proud of where it took me.

He had to step in for so many of his grandchildren. He was the one I turned to when I got pregnant and looking for jobs. Although my grandfather was ill, he still took me job hunting one last time. When we returned home, he gave me a piece of paper and said, "I want you to remember these as you step out in life." On the paper were two Scriptures.

The first one came from Psalm 121:1-2, "I will lift up my eyes to the hills—From whence comes my help? My help *comes* from the Lord, Who made heaven and earth." This Scripture will stay close to my heart for the rest of my life. I will have to rely on this when I cannot look to anyone but the Lord to help bring me through difficult situations. Some of them you will read in this book, but many others were not shared.

The other Scripture came from Romans 8:37, "Yet in all these things we are more than conquerors through Him who loved us." I needed to know about His love from this Scripture. All I ever wanted was to be loved. I also needed to know that I was a conqueror when life tried to conquer me. They were just Scriptures, but they pointed me to my Heavenly Father, who would fill voids left unfulfilled in life. My grandfather left me the greatest gift by pointing me directly to Jesus.

You may have grown up not knowing your father, or not having him in your home. You may have had a father who provided child support, but you had no more of a relationship with him than I did with mine. In God, the fatherless can find compassion. I like how

Hosea 14:3 (AMPC) reads, "For in You [O Lord] the fatherless find love, pity, and mercy." We can always find love with God that our earthly fathers were unable to provide.

Maybe you never had his love and support, because other siblings were favored over you, creating sibling tension. I can truly admire men who show love and support to all of their children and not just some. Perhaps you just couldn't do anything right for your dad, no matter how hard you tried; this caused you to be at war with each other. I realize that some have fathers who provoke them, and this should not be the case.

> "Fathers, do not irritate *and* provoke your children to anger [do not exasperate them to resentment], but rear them [tenderly] in the training *and* discipline and the counsel *and* admonition of the Lord."
> -Ephesians 6:4 (AMPC)

Some of us had earthly fathers who just didn't reflect the character of our heavenly Father God, but we don't have to follow their patterns. This does not have to stop you from being successful in life, or a better parent than what was displayed to you. Philippians 4:19 reads, "And my God shall supply all your need according to His riches in glory by Christ Jesus." According to God's will, there's no need in our life that He cannot supply.

Nothing is impossible for Him, even when we need the love and support of a father. God has people assigned to your life for specific purposes. Sometimes, they may not come through who we think they should. God can use all kinds of people to show us an example of His genuine love.

John 3:16 reads, "For God so loved the world that He gave His only begotten Son, that whoever believes in Him should not perish but have everlasting life." No one, including our earthly father, will ever be able to show us a greater love than this.

The Heart of a Loving Mother

"A woman who fears the Lord is to be praised. Honor her for all that her hands have done, and let her works bring her praise at the city gate." -Proverb 31:30-31 (NIV)

So, *I didn't fully* understand the heart of my loving mother, as a child, until I had to face my own set of personal issues and challenges as a believer, mother, and wife. People looked at how close we were and assumed that it had been like that from the very beginning. Mom knew about this book and told me to tell the truth — the good, the bad, and the ugly. There was nothing ever so ugly that it could destroy my love for her.

We were not perfect and had our share of ups and downs, like some mother and daughter relationships. We saw mothers and daughters who didn't speak to each other for days, or years, due to unresolved issues. We didn't want that to happen to us; therefore, we chose to work on problem situations.

I cannot even imagine driving all the way to Tennessee, while she was alive, to visit others, and never stopping to visit the woman of God who raised me. I realize that some mother and daughter relationships are strained, full of trouble, and often unable to be repaired. But we should never let pride be the reason that stops us from walking in forgiveness with them.

We never wanted to look down on the other, in a coffin, regretting we never took the chance to say, "I'm sorry for whatever I did to you." We said, "I'm sorry" and "Forgive me" to one another whenever needed, even when I got on her nerves, and she got on mines. Before she transitioned to heaven, we had a chance to express those words again. I told her I was sorry for whatever I did as a child or adult, that may have hurt her. She told me to stop it; that all I did was love her, and she was thankful that I was still showing that love. I said it wasn't always shown, but she stopped me, and said the good outweighed the bad; she appreciated everything I've done for her.

I always say that it's the truth we face about ourselves that sets us free. Hopefully, the truth shared may help some mothers and daughters restore and strengthen their relationship, as God did ours because we were not always that close or trouble-free.

I grew up around many alcoholics and people who got high. Mom was one, although I don't know when it started. She married as a teenager and had me when she was sixteen years old. She later gave birth to my brother at eighteen years old. Her first marriage didn't last long, nor would it be her last. It was the start of a tumultuous childhood. She entered another abusive marriage, and I developed much turmoil and fear as a child from that relationship.

Even at such a young age, I felt alone. In my adult years, when God was delivering me, He showed me a vision. I was a toddler, standing on the couch, looking out a big picture window, and crying for my parents. I had not seen them for a while, and I was crying for their return. Where were they? Why did they leave me? Where is my Mom? Those questions followed me into my teen years, along with other problems and issues.

During Mom's second marriage, I remember them always partying, drinking, fussing, and fighting. She tried to be protective of her children, but she could not protect us from the turmoil we encountered in that environment. In kindergarten, I was already tired of the fights witnessed and knew alcohol had a part in it. When other kids brought canned goods to school to feed the needy, I took left-over alcohol from a recent party to give to whoever needed it. I'm sure she was quite surprised and embarrassed when the school called her to come and pick it up.

The confusion, turmoil, and fights would continue; I hated to see my mom beaten. Once, while my stepdad was beating her, I turned on an iron. When it was hot enough, I unplugged it and ran toward him, crying to leave my Mama alone, sticking the metal to his behind. Mom left that marriage, and again we went to live with my aunt. This was the start of being uprooted many times during my childhood, to attend four different elementary schools.

Mom always found jobs so she could provide a roof over our heads. When she worked out of state, we lived with my father's sister. She didn't get any child support, so she would sometimes work two or three part-time jobs to make ends meet. Our physical and material needs were met, but emotionally, we were in need.

Mom finally was able to get her first place. It was a roach-infested garage, fixed up as an apartment. It was all she could afford, so she had it exterminated before we moved in. I wanted to continue to stay with my aunt instead and asked her why we couldn't stay in the Projects a block away. I did not find out this answer until I was an adult. She didn't want us to get stuck in a system to grow up influenced by gangs, drugs, or the like.

I was embarrassed to stay in that garage. The garage was sectioned into a tiny living room with a couch that she slept on, a small bathroom that included enough space for a toilet and sink, but no tub — a silver tub was pulled out for baths — a small stove, fridge and sink for the kitchen, and a separate room with two twin beds for me and my brother. Young, embarrassed, and ashamed, I had to address those feelings later in life. I didn't want the other kids to see me go into an ally to get home. To get home, I cut through her best friend's yard on the next street, whose backside faced the garage. That was the only bad place we lived in, and after that, it was as if she said, "never again." We didn't stay in that place long, but to me, it felt like an eternity.

Later, Mom was able to move us into a two-bedroom apartment next door to her best friend, but not far from that garage. Every time I attended my church in Alabama, I saw an old garage next door to the parking lot. A man lived there, so it always reminded me of when we stayed in one during my childhood.

Mom didn't stay in the apartment long and went on to buy a beautiful three-story house with no job. I couldn't figure out how she was able to do that, but I did later. Luke 2:52 states, "And Jesus increased in wisdom and stature, and in favor with God and men." Throughout her life, she found favor with God and with people in so many areas. This included some job opportunities with the help of those in politics, materialistic things, plenty of food, and some of the best-dressed kids in school, even when she was making minimal wages. These were the good memories, but other things took place during those years also.

The bad and ugly was that we didn't always have her; many things were built on lies told by her, and some things happened to hurt us for years. The damage had already started years before moving into those places.

She went from her parents' home to her in-laws upon my arrival while she was a teenage mother. After the divorces, she began enjoying her life by partying, sometimes at the expense of her children. We were left with family, occasionally with friends of the family, when molestation took place.

When we moved into the house, there were times we were left by ourselves, not knowing where Mom was. I was very protective, caring for my brother while we were in elementary school. We were never left without food or clean clothes. The fridge stayed packed, and we had plenty of clothes.

My brother looked to me as his parent; I must have believed it too. Once, while Mom was whipping him, I yelled, "Leave him alone! You're not his Mama." She looked at me like I had lost my mind. The anger of trying to take care of a child, but yet still a child myself, started to develop into hurt and hatred. When he needed something, I told him to "go ask your Mama." His response was, "I would, but she's never around; you the Mama." He was as hurt as I was, but I wasn't his Mama. I needed her, too, but drinking and the world ways had her.

She had no control over her drinking and disappeared one time for almost two weeks. We had no idea if she was alive or dead because we were told that what goes on in her house, stays in her house. The fears of the repercussion of letting others know she was not home, stopped us from telling. We found out later that she was partying in Detroit as if she forgot she had kids. I wouldn't let my brother have any company, nor did I let my friends know. As far as people knew, she was in the house with her kids.

Friends thought we had the coolest Mom, and we were the kids who had everything that they wanted. We did have a lot of things, but we didn't have Mom. I started driving early, not because I was of age; it was because Mom was drunk and let me. So, I drove her when she was drunk. I drove to deposit money at the bank. I wrote out checks to pay bills. I drove to the store to pick up food.

The more she drank, the more men would appear on the scene. I was young, but I noticed the look of lust in some of their eyes toward me, that shouldn't have been there. So, I developed a hard front to keep men from thinking I was going to put up with molestation from them.

Mom was very friendly, and people loved her. When they described my brother, it was said that he was friendly just like her, but her daughter is something else; she watches people like a hawk. She's not the friendly one. I had to be something else to keep some men at a distance.

I went to family members' homes to get away, but they were households that included more drinking and sometimes fighting. I developed a false responsibility of caring for my brother and mother.

I started making inner vows that I didn't want to be like either of my parents. I judged my Mom, along with my dad, within my heart. I didn't know anything about Luke 6:37, "Judge not, and you shall not be judged. Condemn not, and you shall not be condemned. Forgive, and you will be forgiven."

I was depressed, hating life, and hating what Mom was doing, so I rebelled before high school. By the time I made it to the Sixth grade, I was dating, but not according to my age. Mom said, "You can't date that boy. He is too old for you, and I'm stopping that." I told her to go ahead and try to stop it; "I'll just sneak around like you're doing with all these men." And so, the mother and daughter battle had begun. It's a wonder she didn't slap me, then, from Indiana to Alabama. He was working, almost out of high school, and was soon to be working at the steel mill. That relationship ended when I made it to high school because I didn't want to end up like my parents – young with kids.

From then on, I started excelling in school, planning for a better life. But our battles continued throughout high school until Mom stopped drinking. She saw the hurt in me and my brother, but she saw the hatred in my eyes while I was taking care of her during a drunken episode. She stopped drinking for a while, but it was years before we could start repairing the relationship.

Many other things happened that just cannot be written at this time. I know she was proud when I excelled in school, and for every title or accomplishment achieved. As she started cleaning up her life, she realized that she had children who were hurt by her actions. But there were things she was not ready to deal with. I moved out early with my child, almost repeating a cycle of things she did. I didn't want to be a product of my environment.

We both tried not to deal with the ugly side until she got my daughter for a summer and fell back into drinking. My daughter snuck off to call me to let me know that they were in the car, the adults were drunk, and they had gone off the road into a ditch. She was told not to tell me. Mom had moved to Tennessee at this time, but the next day, I left Indiana to get my daughter. I didn't realize how much anger was still within me that needed to be dealt with. I left Tennessee with my child, telling Mom it would be a while before she saw her again because she would not do to her what you did to us. I didn't think about what drove my Mom to drink then, or while she was raising us. I stopped talking to her, and it tore both of us up. Her best friend, who had always been constant in our life, intervened.

Healing began to take place as we grew in our relationship with Christ. Mom apologized for the hurt she caused, and so did I. There was nothing she wouldn't do for us, but Mom struggled as a single Mom. When we saw her drinking, she was escaping, really, from a troubled life in an unhealthy way.

We had everything materialistic because she never had those things growing up and didn't want the same for her kids. When she disappeared, drunk, she had no control, but she thought she was protecting us by not allowing us to see her in a worse state. She said what made her quit drinking the first time was the hatred she saw in my eyes. What made her quit the second time was the hatred she began to see in her own eyes.

Joel 2:25 reads, "So I will restore to you the years that the swarming locust has eaten." As we both let God continue to heal us within, we saw an acceleration in our relationship — the years were restored that the enemy tried to steal, kill, and destroy. The wisdom of God began to replace the foolishness of the enemy, and an intimacy developed that existed for the rest of our lives.

I saw a woman of God who blessed and forgave those who spitefully used and persecuted her. I saw people who didn't love or care for her and learned from her example. I often asked her toward the end how she could do this, knowing how they felt. Her response was, "I don't have a heaven or hell to put them in, and neither do you. No matter how they treat you, give them to Jesus, and let the Lord do what only He can do. No matter what you go through, give it to the Lord." That was her response until she left this earth.

Maybe you're at a crossroads with your Mom, or she is not alive today. Deuteronomy 32:11 reads, "As an eagle stirs up its nest, Hovers over its young, Spreading out its wings, taking them up, Carrying them on its wings . . ."

God uses some situations to teach us how to fly in life. No matter what we go through, He's right there, close to us, ready to help. In those places where we fail or fall, He is there to bring us to a safe place.

When Scripture tells us that "all things work together for good to those who love God," it does not mean just because we love God, all things that happen will be good. How can all the messes in our life be worked out for good? Only God can reveal and work together the good out of seemingly impossible situations in our life.

Bad things happen to good people, and sometimes bad environments can destroy innocent lives, but we don't have to let our environment negatively influence our future. God has a way of using everything we went through and works it out for good.

Even if your relationship was strained with another female who influenced your life, leaving you hurt, give it to the Lord. He's a specialist in dealing with our hurts and our hearts. The Bible tells us God heals the brokenhearted and binds up their wounds. The only pains or trauma we hold on to are those we refuse to let Him have and heal. Choose today to walk in forgiveness and see God work all things together for your good.

Unexpected Blessings from Unexpected People and Places

> "And my God shall supply all your need according to His riches in glory by Christ Jesus." -Philippians 4:19

God has a way of using people and places to bring unexpected blessings into our lives. There's an African proverb that says, "It takes a village to raise a child." I heard this statement throughout my life. Usually, it meant a community of people who looked out for children, other than theirs, allowing them to grow in a safe and healthy environment.

We don't have to be children for God to send us places or give us a community of people to help, teach, or assist us in life. They're usually blessings in disguise, people sent by God from our village. I would have a village specifically sent by God to help me soar in many areas. Those people we think we lack in life can come through the blessings of others to fulfill a divine purpose.

God would allow aunts from both of my parents' families to display His love to a troubled child. On my father's side, my aunt was a source I ran to until the day she died. I thought I was one of her kids and her favorite niece. I was quite surprised at her funeral to learn that she had a lot of favorite nieces, nephews, and other people who felt the same. She had a way of making us all feel special.

I lived with her during some of the most traumatic years. She provided not only love, but also guidance, correction, and counseling. She was the glue to tie me to my father's side of the family. All it took was one person to show true love from that side of the family for me to connect with them.

My mother's sisters would make me feel special also, and they impacted my life greatly. Sometimes, when ugly things happen to us, we don't see ourselves as the Lord sees us. We might even see ourselves as ugly, until we receive deliverance and counseling. But my mom's sisters always saw me differently from the way I saw myself.

Psalm 139:14 reads, "I will praise You, for I am fearfully *and* wonderfully made; Marvelous are Your works, And *that* my soul knows very well." My mom's sisters contributed to the part of making me see my beauty. I always thought I was ugly growing up, and their love caused me to see my beauty. They made me feel like I was a queen. I entered queen pageants in high school and won, but the confidence wavered when I ran for Miss Indiana. Even with wavering confidence, I was still recognized to get an award.

It was years before I truly learned that God has made everything beautiful in its own time. These aunts had beautiful and successful daughters, but they still found time to invest in my life. One aunt pushed me to excel in school, to go further than they did at the time. The other aunt had me modeling all over the city of Gary, contributing to outfits I wore that were truly unique at the time. These same aunts helped me adjust prior to the transition of my mom. They always were around. This part of the village help provided the love that I so needed in my life.

I received a lot of protection and guidance from people God placed in my village, also. A male friend that Mom dated from Chicago provided protection. He knew the turmoil we were going through and always felt I had too much responsibility on me for a child. He was there to bring some balance into our lives. When he was around, I was able to do things children are supposed to be doing. I didn't have to cook because he did it. I had my tasks, but they were reduced when he was around. When Mom disappeared, sometimes with other men, he came and watched us until she came back. We saw and felt his protection. Psalm 91:4 (AMPC) says, "[Then] He will cover you with His pinions, and under His wings shall you trust *and* find refuge; His truth *and* His faithfulness are a shield and a buckler." I'll always love him for the love and protection he showed us like a father figure. I didn't know how much of a blessing he was until I got older and read about the abuse that goes on with some women's boyfriends and their children.

I also saw a different type of protection with one of my high school instructors. He was a father figure to many of us there, because we didn't have fathers in our homes, nor did we have a relationship with them. I remember going to another school's prom on the same day that I was to receive some awards at my senior banquet. He knew Mom couldn't do a lot financially at that time. She had quit drinking and made some changes in her life. I wanted mom to have flowers. He ordered her flowers, and they were presented to her as she picked up my awards. Mom told me it was one of her happiest days. That friendship continued even after high school. He saw, counseled, and guided me through some traumatic adult years. With this part of the village, not only was love showed, but protection and guidance were given.

God used many people on my job to help push me into my career destiny. My supervisor ended up being a great supportive friend. She met me as a young single mother, and we have remained friends over the years. Under her supervision, I was trained right and advanced quickly. She made sure we were being trained for future opportunities, so if a position came available, we could apply. She helped a lot of people shift to the next level, although we didn't know it at the time. Coming into that job, I had to wait on others to finish before I could do my job. She never wasted time but had me cross-train — helping others to finish their work.

The woman she set me up with ended up training me for every position I had in my career. We remained friends, also. She would not let me quit. She told me, "You know you're the cream of the crop, and we're going to help you to rise." There were times that I messed up jobs. She said, "It's okay; now you're going to learn how to correct them." We were in a bank environment and correcting meant closing files that people could not access, which meant angry customers back then.

When I wanted to quit, she stepped in as trainer and coach, way back then. There were times that she coached me through my studies at Purdue. She used job references without giving me the answers. Then she asked me how I would handle this at work. When I told her my answer, she said, "Now relate it to the schoolwork." When I left the state, due to promotion, she felt like she was seeing her baby move away.

There was another co-worker who made an impact in my life; we also remained friends. She was older, so she was able to help me through some foolish spending. The financial wisdom I learned from her helped me to get out of debt and save money. Most people, when they have money problems, want others to give them the money to get out of their hardship instead of the wisdom to learn from it.

She sat down with me, and we went over my income and outgoing expenses. She had me track everything I spent, so I could see the wasteful spending areas. She gave me saving tips.

After her financial wisdom, I was able to get out of debt and save money. Hebrews 6:10 (NIV) reads, "God is not unjust; He will not forget your work and the love you have shown Him as you have helped His people and continue to help them." These ladies helped me reach greatness with skill sets that continue to follow me from state to state. This part of my village provided love, support, and coaching for divine financial and career destinies.

Many pastors and people in ministry helped develop me into the minister I am today. Jeremiah 3:15 says, "And I will give you shepherds according to My heart, who will feed you with knowledge and understanding." I was divinely placed under their leadership for the purposes of God. Each one has played a part in the development of my Christian walk. I believe I have only seen a tip of what God wants to do in my life, through their investments in me. The wisdom and knowledge they imparted not only affected my life, but those I come into contact with.

Under my Indiana Pastor's leadership, I came into a lifestyle of living in holiness. Under the leadership of my Pennsylvania Pastor, I really became a student of the Bible and applied principles learned to my life. Under my Georgia pastors' leadership, I gained freedom, healing, deliverance, and much training that will be used for ministry purposes. Then, under my Alabama pastor's leadership, I was challenged to let my gifts come out of the box. Now, under my current bishop's leadership, he has gently led the prophet out of hiding, from the cave into new ministry opportunities. Those opportunities came with additional new challenges. He has assisted me through some strong spiritual warfare attacks and fed me the Word of God over and over to strengthen and encourage me along the way.

Additional people, ministers, Ministering Bible College, and Dance School came along to provide additional training in Praise and Worship training, deliverance, counseling, and ministry ordination opportunities. This part of my village has provided love, support, inspiration, ministry, training, deliverance, spiritual guidance, and direction.

God allowed me to birth a beautiful daughter, who has become my greatest unexpected blessing. Not because of the way she came, but how she ended up saving my life. I didn't know how much she would actually impact my life until she became an adult. Psalm 127:3 reads, "Behold, children *are* a heritage from the Lord, The fruit of the womb *is* a reward." As they placed her in my arms, I was holding a precious life that I was now responsible for. That responsibility has kept me holding on to life.

I loved her dearly, even from the time she was in my womb. I didn't have an ultrasound to determine her gender forty-something years ago. I just knew I had a girl, and her name was picked out early in my pregnancy. I had concerns as a young mother and wondered if I would be able to care for her in the way she should be. I would learn the answer to this over the years.

I didn't want her to experience the hurt or turmoil I encountered in life. She would have her own share of struggles to overcome due to the pitfalls of her parents. Sometimes when dysfunction is not dealt with, we can pass it down to our children unknowingly. Did I raise her in the Lord? I didn't until I came into a revelation of Christ in my life.

She gave her life to Christ at an early age. She declared, as a teen, "What happened to you and your Mom, I don't want happening to me." My assignment was to pour into her life Godly principles needed to be successful. Proverb 18:21 reads, "Death and life are in the power of the tongue, And those who love it will eat its fruit." As parents, we have to be careful about what we say, especially with our children. I've seen parents' gossip with their children, raising them to do the same. Gossip can't save your life when you're in turmoil, like the Word of God. If all you can do is teach them those words or actions of death, there will come a time that you reap what was sown into them.

There came a time that she would pour God's Word of life back into me when life overwhelmed me because I fed her the living Word of God. I've had the opportunity to reap some great benefits from her over the years, and they have not ceased. Her paths are different from mine, but she is successful in what God has called her to do. She observed me during many unhealed moments and in some of my hardest years that could have brought her trauma.

In many prayers, I spoke life over her more than I did myself. My words echoed back into my ears when she has had to do the same to me as an adult. The love I showed my mom returned to me more than double from her. I am loved, respected, honored, pampered, spoiled, and treated like a queen by this blessed woman of God, that includes great gifts. Some of those great gifts include five grandchildren she birthed that will continue the bloodline.

She never knew how God used her so many times during appropriate moments to be a blessing. As I poured into her, she also poured into others assigned to her hands. I'm just blessed and honored that God assigned her to my womb, because she will always be my greatest unexpected blessing in life!

Why did I share these testimonies about unexpected blessings? Revelations 12:11 reads, "And they overcame him by the blood of the Lamb and by the word of their testimony." What challenges we overcome or testimonies we share in life can help someone else overcome theirs.

We can become so distracted by what the enemy is doing in our lives. In those times of turmoil, we may forget or miss the blessings God provided through people or places. Blessings may not always come through a family member. There were many friends that are a part of my village that helped along the way.

Many of you may have experienced God's blessings through the hands of friends or associates. God has specific people He has assigned to bless us. 2 Corinthians 9:8 reads, "And God *is* able to make all grace abound toward you, that you, always having all sufficiency in all *things*, may have an abundance for every good work."

Sometimes people get angry at others that they think should provide them with something. God will send blessings through people to give you what's needed, even though they may not be family members or the people you expected. Take a look into your life and notice God's placement of people to meet a specific need. We all have them throughout our life and should let brotherly love continue through us.

Scripture tells us in Hebrews 13:2, "Do not forget to entertain strangers, for by so doing some have unwittingly entertained angels." Who are the angels in your life? We can receive unexpected blessings from unexpected people and places. But God also expects us to be a blessing to others, so they can see His love flow through us.

Remember this when you think about blessings in life — are you a "giver" or a "taker"? "Givers" always give their time, resources, love, loyalty, or commitment, regardless of what it costs them, what is done to them, or said about them. They sometimes end up receiving more through unexpected blessings, from unexpected people and places. "Takers" always take because they feel they are entitled, or it's owed to them.

Which one are you? Can you bless others without expecting to receive something back? Luke 6:38 tells us, "Give, and it will be given to you: good measure, pressed down, shaken together, and running over will be put into your bosom. For with the same measure that you use, it will be measured back to you."

As you serve Christ and others, let God's blessings show you that you are a blessing to others also.

When God Says Move

What do you do when life takes you through wilderness experiences, one after another? You cried so many tears until you believed there's no more left to shed, then you're left feeling weary and faint.

Psalm 30:5 says, "Weeping may endure for the night, but joy comes in the morning." What do you do when you discover the night has turned into days, weeks, months, and years? How long is the night, LORD? You prayed and prayed and prayed for God to move all of the wildernesses, pain, and frustrations far away, but they still managed to appear and linger. Now God is telling you to not only move away from the things that have frustrated you, but physically move to a new location, far away from your comfort zone.

Amazing how God will have you move away from things, people, or places when you want to stay; yet has you stay in places that make you want to quickly run away. I discovered that the most dangerous place could become the safest place — inside the will of God. Yet, the safest place can become the most dangerous place outside of the will of God. When God says move, there's no sense fighting Him or His command. When God says move, there are blessings and lessons to learn attached to those moves.

My natural moves in life include Gary, Indiana; Monroeville, Pennsylvania; Dunwoody, Georgia; and Opelika, Alabama. It included some spiritual moves, career moves, and movement among relationships. People I thought would be lifelong friends, ended up being seasonal friends for God's specific purposes. People I thought would be seasonal friends remained around, even till today, fulfilling another specific assignment from God. People I thought would be faithful, ended up betraying my trust. People I thought were trustworthy, proved to be unfaithful. Family I thought would love and celebrate me, ended up tolerating me instead. But God still moves. . . and will move us or others.

God has a way of using "movement," even with statements in life. I have always heard the statement, "Blood is thicker than water" from many, especially in my adult life. That statement has caused me to ponder on its truth and untruth when wronged against. If a blood relative has wronged an individual who is not blood, will they also be confronted with their wrong by the person who is their blood? Movement in relationships can address these issues.

The "moves" to different locations revealed people who thought differently from where I grew up. The "moves" also revealed those of the family of faith, who appeared closer than some family. I heard statements like, "Nobody will ever do for or be there for you like family." Proverbs 18:24 says, "A man *who* has friends must himself be friendly, But there is a friend *who* sticks closer than a brother." I always say, "Thank you, Lord," when there has been a bad family experience, and true friends came to the rescue. Statements like these can be false, because our family has "friends" who have been more like family, being present during some of the roughest times.

Not everyone has or marry into a family who's there for them. I believe God considers these individuals and gives them what or who is needed in their life. For those who do not have the support of their family, God may move others across their paths to show or give what they need the most. All of my "moves" in life reflect this, also. Each "move" in the natural realm had their share of pluses and minuses. Ecclesiastes 3:1 reads, "To everything *there* is a season, A time for every purpose under heaven . . ." God knows the seasons, times, and purposes for each move in our life, although we might not know it at the time.

I was born and raised in Gary, Indiana. In the midst of the turmoil, there still was a lot of love, support, spiritual foundations, and career development preparation. Although I had my share of hurts and disappointments there, Gary was home. God definitely started speaking there, prophetically, and in dreams. I did not understand this until years later. I always knew that God was going to move me, and I believed Atlanta was going to be a place I move to.

In 1991, God had me accelerate with my training, but I could not understand why. I was still working full-time; He had me take full-time classes at Purdue. At the time, I was working three or four days, twelve-hour shifts. I was able to switch with others to attend classes. It was a lot of work because I was also raising my daughter.

Years earlier, in the eighties, I took an entry-level position on the operations side of the IT department and worked my way up, through on-the-job training. I was trying to get into the computer programming side, and the Purdue classes would help me in that area. I didn't see how it was going to be possible while carrying a full load of classes while working fulltime.

In December, right before Christmas, God instructed me to pack the Christmas tree for a move. I didn't know much about the Prophetic then, but I thought I would be moving to a new apartment.

I can remember listening to a pastor out of Chicago on TV around that time. He started prophesying about a change that was coming for some of those watching in the area. I was ironing and stopped to watch the service. It was like he was preaching directly to me. He prophesied about how God was getting ready to move the people who were listening to the east, then south, and then south, again, because of the souls assigned to their hands. He spoke about many who were getting ready to lose jobs as they were going into the next year.

In January 1992, I found out that our bank was bought out and that we would be out of a job with that bank. In March 1992, I had a pastor prophesy that God was getting ready to move me to another city, in another state, and it would happen fast! Now, I was concerned. I was taking a full load at Purdue, and my boss had me entered into an intense company program that allowed me to be relocated if I passed it.

The company could only select around twelve people to take that program at a time. It included about ten weeks of onsite work and about two weeks of work in Little Rock, Arkansas. In Arkansas, we were in class from early morning until after midnight, Monday through Saturday. I was swamped with my job, Purdue classes, and the company training. I didn't think I would be able to pass any of them, nor have a job. I made the Dean's List, did my job, and completed the company training, all in a five-month period.

I dreamed that I moved to a city where the downtown was surrounded by rivers. I really wanted it to be Atlanta, so I asked someone if downtown Atlanta had rivers around it. I found out that it didn't. Gary was definitely used to develop and train me for career moves; however, I would later learn that my spiritual foundation was also going in another direction, for God's purpose.

Before the job ended in Gary, I interviewed for a computer programming position, located in downtown Pittsburgh. When I drove through the tunnel headed to downtown, it was déjà vu when I stared at the exact same sight that was in my dream. The rivers surrounded downtown. God had me take the job that summer in 1992. He moved me east to Pennsylvania, then south to Georgia, and south again to Alabama, just like the preacher prophesied on TV that day.

My time in the Pittsburgh area was only about three years. God had shown me that, also, and I was happy with that time frame. Ecclesiastes 3 mentions, "A time to build up" and "A time to gain." I was being built up spiritually in one area, yet gained skill sets needed for my next move. But my time there brought new feelings. While Gary represented a comfort zone, now I was in a very uncomfortable place. Since God was leading me here, I didn't have the network of support from family and friends in the beginning. In fact, I had no family or knew anyone there. God provided a friend network that was truly a blessing.

On the relocation trip, to find a place to live, God led me to my new church home first. I was planning to look for a church home following the move. That was not going to happen, according to the Lord's plan. I'm reminded of this every time I read Jeremiah 29:11 (NIV), "For I know the plans I have for you," declares the LORD, "plans to prosper you and not to harm you, plans to give you hope and a future." I had a church home and was having a hard time deciding on my top two choices to live. Both were beautiful, but God led me to take the second choice, when I really wanted the first one. I had been learning to follow God's lead way back in Gary, and I continued it in Pennsylvania.

On the one hand, Pittsburgh came with new opportunities that were great for my career and a few other surprises. On the other hand, I encountered some hurtful discrimination from a client who didn't like women in authority over him; he definitely didn't want a black one. There were around two hundred workers, but only about five blacks. It's not that I didn't experience it in the Gary area, because I did . . . also in the workplace. He tried to set me up for failure, but I entered a time of praying without ceasing on that job. Since I had trusted God with this move, I trusted him to resolve the problem through prayer. It did backfire on him, but God always had me in prayer. He was developing my prayer walk and taking it up a notch, differently from the way I prayed in Gary.

The spiritual level for me was like a combination of being in Junior High and High School. I was in the right church, loving the teachings and worship there. Although my time there was short, God continued to develop me in my career and spiritual life. On the jobs, systems that were crashing were assigned to me; I didn't know how to fix them until I went to sleep at night. He always gave the solutions in dreams, waking me up to write it down. At the job, I keyed what He gave me, and it worked every time.

We were there several months before discovering that my daughter was behind in that school district. They were giving her a chance to see if the learning center could catch her up within a certain time frame. I needed a miracle because the amount to pay for this was expensive. A card came in the mail, with a key to my first-choice apartment. It said, "You can live here rent-free for a year, if your key fits." I asked true prayer warriors to pray I get the apartment, because I still had to pay for my daughter's extra training. Our key did not fit the door to the apartment, but they let us in and left us. We prayed, sang, and thanked God like it was our apartment.

They mailed out seven hundred keys, but the winning key never showed up. They had a drawing and . . . guess who won the apartment, rent-free for a year? I paid for her tuition and was almost debt-free. In our relationship with the Lord, nothing is impossible with Him. We were there for almost two more years until the job ended in 1995. I was Atlanta bound!

The Atlanta area was where I always wanted to live. It was a great place for successful African Americans, and I wanted a part of that. All of the previous moves were due to job losses that relocated me to the next state. The Georgia move was not the best for my career, but I worked with some great co-workers. Family and friends who were living there helped with the transition.

The move this time was more spiritual. God spoke to my spirit; He was going to put me among some new brothers and sisters. I was ready to be around these new brothers and sisters in Christ. Like before, God picked the church while I was actually living in Pennsylvania. When I visited the church that He picked, I was quite surprised. The pastors and the congregation were mostly white. This was a different set of brothers and sisters than what I had expected. I was always apart of black ministries. I had stepped into purpose and didn't even know it. I learned what all those dreams, visions, and prophetic revelations meant. It was home for about ten years.

There were opportunities to meet many wonderful people within and outside of the ministry, from all over the world. It became a training ground, similar to college, or so it seemed. I was definitely being prepared for ministry with the Apostolic, the Prophetic, Deliverances, Miracles, Prophetic Dance ministry, workshops, conferences, and other great training. It was an environment that I didn't want to leave. I married there, and then God put an end to that season, like a mother eagle preparing to teach her eaglets how to fly. It was time to spread my wings and soar above in another area.

When God made it clear to move to Alabama, it was a move I had been fighting against for years. He ended the IT career, with no open-door of opportunities in Georgia. By this time, I had been experiencing things within the marriage that I didn't want to deal with. I cried so much, and then God showed me a vision of a crying child. The parent held the child's hand in the vision, but the child kicked, cried, and screamed, "I don't want to go! I don't want to go! Please! Please!" The child was trying to go in the opposite direction while being gently pulled by the parent toward the wilderness. God told me, "This child is you."

I was fighting purpose. Scripture tells us Jesus was led by the Spirit into the wilderness to be tempted by the devil. Who wants more wilderness experiences in life? I had enough of that. If the other states were like school and college, I had now entered boot camp for war, encountering high levels of spiritual warfare. This wilderness produced much hurt, betrayal, deception, rejections, lies, and spiritual attacks. I had to face everything I had heard about . . . like Jezebel and different types of witchcraft spirits. I had to draw strength from years of preparation in Indiana, Pennsylvania, and Georgia. God dropped a plumb line to help me remain weighed down in Christ. I attended the School of Ministering Art Bible College in Georgia and was ordained as a minister and a prophet. Years later, I joined my church in Alabama. The pastor, ministry, and teachings helped me get back to being rooted and focused on the paths in a right relationship with God. I also got ordained as a minister there.

All of these moves fulfilled part of my purpose. Some states, I loved, and some I disliked. I had to face the truth about why I disliked them. The truth was, I didn't like what I experienced in those places. The truth sets us free. When I faced truth, I realized the blessings of those places. I met some wonderful people assigned to my life by God. Even with what the enemy has tried to do in my life by bringing turmoil, I'm still standing in Christ Jesus.

God is holding me up, just like He's holding you with His righteous right hand! There's power in that hand. Many may be reading this and fighting against the moves God desires you to take.

What mountain of trials is keeping you from moving when God says to move?

Perhaps the Lord is telling you the same thing He told Moses and all of Israel, "You have stayed long enough at this mountain." When He tells you to move, Psalm 32:8 reads, "I will instruct you and teach you in the way you should go; I will guide you with My eye." We serve a God we can trust with all of our heart. We never have to be fearful of the places He is leading us to, even if we encounter bumps in the road along the way.

He has promised to direct our paths. His paths always lead us to the prize. Philippians 3:14 says, "I press on toward the goal for the prize of the upward call of God in Christ Jesus." God desires for you to finish this race well. People may not always be there during the times you make those moves, but God will never leave you or forsake you. There's a God-given task He is waiting for you to fulfill, and it involves movements on your part. Will you, now, move when God says move?

Blended Family, not Blending

> "Behold, how good and how pleasant it is for brethren to dwell together in unity!" -Psalm 133:1 (AMPC)

Dysfunction is not new in relationships or families. It existed in relationships throughout the Bible. It was there, beginning with the very first family mentioned, when Cain killed Abel. It was there when "Miriam and Aaron spoke against Moses because of the Ethiopian woman whom he had married." This was a dysfunction of dissension that caused Miriam to become leprous.

It was there among Joseph and his brothers who had different mothers, but the same father, Israel (Jacob). Scripture tells us about Joseph and his brothers in Genesis 37:4, "When his brothers saw that their father loved him more than any of them, they hated him and could not speak a kind word to him." Their hatred caused them to throw Joseph in a pit, pulled him out, and sold him to the Ishmaelites. Dysfunction was in the house that broke Jacob's heart; it was many years before he saw Joseph again.

Even King David had a dysfunctional family with and among his children. His eldest son, Amnon, ended up raping his virgin half-sister Tamar. King David got angry, but the Bible didn't say a thing about him punishing or doing anything to Amnon for the rape.

Tamar's full brother, Absalom, avenged her rape by killing Amnon. Absalom later came against his own father, declared himself King, and slept with his father's concubines. Could it be a dysfunction in his heart against King David, for not dealing with the rape of his sister?

What do you do when dysfunction is in the house and not dealt with? Many families can point out sins of dysfunction in someone else's life, when they are a part of their blended family, yet hold a plank to their eyes to ignore the ones in their natural blood family. Not only does it appear in our natural family, but it's often hard to find yourself a part of a blended family, only to discover that you all are not blending well due to some type of dysfunction.

My life has consisted of being a part of blended families, due to my parents' divorce when I was a young girl, and their involvement with others. I have observed dysfunction when spouses let family members attack or spiritually assassinate their mate's character. They didn't try to protect, defend, or support them, leaving them feeling like an outsider, unloved and unvalued. I remember listening to a sermon when the speaker said, "If you let someone else attack your spouse, they are also attacking you!"

I've seen children replace stepparents, leaving the closeness undeveloped between them. Even as a stepchild and adult, someone from the blended family always lets you know that "blood was always thicker." I took that to mean that I would not be looked at the same, like the blood relative to them.

I know that some blended families can have great relationships without issues, but this is not my story. I've only observed a few good ones that appeared issue free. We all have issues; no one is totally issue free. The majority of the ones I've seen encounter some bumps in the road and had to work through some type of dysfunction. But when those bumps are not dealt with, it builds walls between individuals, leaving them unable to communicate about the issues that exist.

One of the reasons I loved my father's sister, my aunt, so much was because she showed love to many others. Even when her brothers divorced and remarried others with blended families, she had a way of making everyone feel special and loved throughout her life. If her brothers' marriages didn't last, her relationship did with those blended families. She didn't divorce them because her brothers did.

Sometimes, when a divorce takes place, people take the side of their biological family member, even if they are wrong. The members of the blended family can sometimes be ignored. If you are not a part of the natural family, they divorce, not only the mate, but that mate's children. Some children never understand why they no longer can play or see cousins, only to be told that they're not your real cousins, aunts, uncles, or family anyway.

I can remember when my uncle was killed by his second wife. I used to love seeing this particular uncle and to hear him sing with my mom. I remember him always being happy, but the wife being sad. I didn't know he was using her as a punching bag, and she also suffered from emotional abuse. I just saw her sad all of the time. They had no kids together, but I remember enjoying the times I spend with her children.

After the killing, I could sense a lot of hatred being directed toward them, but not from my aunt. I knew everyone was upset about my uncle's death, but I had heard things as a child. I didn't understand everything I heard. Years later, I asked my aunt how she was able to still show love to them back then. She made it clear that "you never truly know what goes on in a marriage or a home.

Just because they were not your natural blood cousins does not mean I'm not going to stand up for what is right."

She knew what it was like to be treated differently with abuse, as part of a blended family, as a stepchild and a wife. She reached out to many blended families, even on my mom's side, who had endured spousal abuse or were treated differently by their blended family. They were helped by the love she gave them. When her talk ended with me about my uncle, she said, "You know him as a loving uncle. I know him as a loving brother, but I also knew he beat the heck out of her. Although it was wrong for her to kill him, it was also wrong for him to keep beating her. She knew him as a wife abuser; everyone has a breaking point."

My aunt stood up for righteousness, even when people did wrong in the family, including me. I never encountered another woman like her who would do the same with a blended family. I have met women who were abused by mates in some way, and still support the abusers in their family, instead of the blended family member. My aunt helped blend families with love, leading many away from dysfunction. I'm not saying her life was free from dysfunction, but she was free to help many in theirs. The turmoil of my uncle's death caused his blended family to move away; we never saw them again.

In blended families, there may be stepparents who never embrace stepchildren, and stepchildren who may never embrace stepparents. There may be division between in-laws and spouse's mates and vice versus. There may be blended families who are never celebrated, but merely tolerated, due to marrying into that family. There may be blended family members who are shunned and rejected. Rejection used to always bother me when I was ignored and not included. If you really want to include a person, you go directly to them and not through others. It was not until I came into an awareness that rejection is not always about you, but about issues people may have with you. Sometimes, the issues can be on your side, or it may even be on theirs.

I had my own feelings to overcome, being a part of a blended family. The truth I faced about my own life sets me free. I married into a family with many anointing and gifting. They include pastors, a bishop, an apostle, prophets, ministers, singers, talented musicians, and a songwriter, those with successful military careers or natural interior design skillsets, great cooks, and successful business owners. I recognize theirs, yet felt mine were not recognized in the same way. I didn't believe they truly knew me, and I definitely didn't know them like I should, like family.

I always thought that I would marry into a loving family that would embrace my daughter and me as much as they embraced each other. We felt embraced by some family members, but not always by others. We came from different backgrounds, so of course, we looked at things, people and life differently. Their family network seemed to be built around their relationship and time with each other. My network was different and a little smaller, including friends along with family. They like doing everything together as a family unit; that includes family trips, holidays, and birthdays, mainly for the siblings. I wanted to be free to do what God wanted me to do, and not in captivity to the demands of others like I was when in bondage.

I began to have a problem when it seemed like decisions were made that didn't include or allow my input — like I didn't have a choice, and the sisters would have the final say. My experiences with abuse, control, and manipulation from others caused walls to go up early in our relationship. I felt their control over their brother superseded choices for our marriage, and many times they did. This caused me to feel smothered and controlled, also. I noticed things that appeared to be one-sided in the relationship, but never told them.

When two people married, there are usually additional families to spend holidays or time with. I missed spending time with mine. To me, it was assumed that most of the important holidays were planned as if we had to do it because they always did it that way. By the second or third year, I wanted to split time and embrace my family also for holidays, birthdays, and special occasions.

There were occasions I would have loved to see my in-laws share with me as I had shared theirs in the beginning. We shared occasions only on their side. They didn't attend my daughter's college graduation, which I understood because it was about four hours away. I couldn't understand them not coming to the house for the graduation party (since they go to Atlanta sometimes) as they had done for everyone else's. I could even understand them not attending her wedding or her babies' showers because they were held out of town. But I heard about events they attended for others out of town, so why couldn't they do the same for me. I had to let it go.

I totally felt like an outsider and did not blend. I experienced the death of a father, stepfather, and brother, and yet, they were not there either. I gave a retirement party for my mom. One family member attended with the friend who took pictures. Sometimes, it seemed if one person didn't show, none came. I had to deal with the hurts from that, and thought, I'm not really their family member, anyway. This was a statement I heard while young.

I slowly pulled away from family events because I felt the family was not blending with me at all. I can't say that we truly conquered all issues that may have existed among us. It was more like ignoring talks about unresolved issues, in the hope that they would go away. Walls to communication had gone up over the years, so everyone pretended that everything was okay. It even spread to the next generation.

No one wanted to deal with confrontation; it caused tension in our relationship. I do believe there were hurt feelings all around because of things never discussed. This was an area God had me deal with inner healing through counseling and deliverance. He also used it for ministering purposes down the line when I didn't expect it. Do we love each other? I believe we do, but we just didn't communicate when certain things needed to be resolved.

Life has a way of changing your outlet about your feelings or how to look at people. God will have you release people and walk in forgiveness, so you can see the blessing of being connected, even when they are family, but not blending. I saw the family gathered together to support me in the death of my mom, and their support was greatly appreciated.

God desires for us to dwell in unity, but based on our background with blended families, we might have to work at it. If hurt is involved, you must release hurt or bitterness, and walk in forgiveness. God can use blended family members in our lives to do just what it says in Proverb 27:17 (NIV), "As iron sharpens iron, so one person sharpens another." God may use others to sharpen us, or He may use us to sharpen them.

Who is God using to sharpen you into His finished product? He may use many of our blended families to rub off the rough edge of our life. Usually, He is teaching all parties involved about something that He desires to do in our lives, but many times, we may not see their purposes at first. Even if it is true that you're not loved by some, God can bless you in the midst of those who don't show love to you.

Psalm 23:5 says, "You prepare a table before me in the presence of my enemies; You anoint my head with oil; My cup runs over." The great part about sitting at the table in the presence of your enemies . . . God can still anoint you in front of them! They cannot stop your cup from running over when God is filling that cup. They cannot stop the blessings or favor upon your life to succeed. They may even think you are not all that, but God made you a conqueror to excel, even within a blended family. He placed you among them to fulfill part of your purpose. God may have used some of your blended family to realign you to walk through a door He has opened. If He has opened the door, walk through it with boldness and confidence, and let your gift make room for you even among blended families!

Broken Covenant

"So then, they are no longer two but one flesh. Therefore what God has joined together, let not man separate." -Matthew 19:6

What happens when you wholeheartedly love someone, but you find out that they didn't love you the same? You soon discover that everything you had was built on lies and deceit. How do you stay when everything inside of you (caused by weapons of spiritual warfare, anxieties, life problems, setbacks, worries, or fears), is so overwhelming that you just want to quit? Now you want to walk away from jobs, assignments, relationships, family members, or even from churches due to a broken covenant.

Have you ever experienced so much pain in your heart, that as you fell on your knees in prayer, it felt like you couldn't breathe because of the pain? Not only does it seem like you were stabbed in the back, but a knife appeared to be stabbed into your heart. How do you find hope in the midst of the biggest storm, experienced by a broken covenant? The pain can leave open wounds, sometimes taking a long time to heal. Have you had the feeling of a hole in your heart so big that only God could fill it? Maybe the hole seemed like you were in the pit of hell, and only God could pull you out. How do you bounce back from the wounds and hurts that have affected your spirit and your soul through a broken covenant?

When the covenant has been broken by those closest to your heart, you're left wondering how you can ever trust the individuals again. When you have broken trust, you will definitely have a broken relationship. A broken covenant can come in many forms. There are times it may happen on the job, among employees or employers. There are times it can happen among trusted friends or associates like Judas did to Jesus. Even in church or ministry, people can get close enough to do the most damage. I wouldn't call them true friends. They were close associates, but even they can be used to fulfill God's purpose.

A broken covenant may even be a part of your assignment. What do you do when turmoil and tribulation are raining upon your life because you discover your assignment included a broken covenant? Although you may have said, "God, I'll do Your will," now you discover it's a "will or an assignment" that you just don't even understand; you feel it's too hard, you don't like it, and you want someone else to go do it as Moses did. Maybe, you just don't feel God's peace or strength to complete your assignment, because of a broken covenant.

Many covenant relationships have been destroyed by unfaithfulness, betrayal, adultery, or infidelity. If you commit the sin in secrecy, to break a covenant, you still did it openly before the Lord and the enemy. Then that sin allowed the enemy legal entrance into that relationship to steal, kill, and destroy it at his designated time. Even if he has to "outwait you" and he can, in order to do the most damage to your marriage or covenant relationships, the enemy has had many years of experience to use it against you. At the appropriate time, he can bring damage and brokenness against you, or those you're in a covenant with. When Jesus was tempted in the wilderness by Satan, Luke 4:13 says, "Now when the devil had ended every temptation, he departed from Him until an opportune time." If the enemy waited for the opportune time for Jesus, he surely waits for an opportune time to get to us.

You may find yourself surrounded by the comfortless type of friends that Job had during a broken covenant. They are people who come with religious sayings that just don't seem to bring any comfort or peace to your heart. You may smile and pretend, anyway, as they do, but you know that some of these people like contributing to your brokenness. Because they think you the cause, they really don't see your pain or how severe the storm is from a broken covenant!

Jeremiah 8:22 reads, "*Is there* no balm in Gilead?" Well, I never have been to Gilead, except for the reading of the Bible. But I do believe that Jesus is our balm in Gilead, to heal brokenness created in our hearts by pain from others. His blood can heal the deepest wound to restore us and make us whole.

A broken covenant can even lead people to make a choice to sin. We all will have an opportunity to make right or wrong decisions, and we all will face temptations and weaknesses. 1 Corinthians 10:13 reads, "No temptation has overtaken you except such as is common to man; but God is faithful, who will not allow you to be tempted beyond what you are able, but with the temptation will also make the way of escape, that you may be able to bear it." Many believe sin is pleasurable for a season. The devil can use that season to entrap us in, or by our sin.

Many don't want their flesh purified because they may not have a reverent fear of God. They may not want to escape sin, but endure it to the fullness, because they believe there will be no consequences. There are always consequences and sometimes at a great cost. It may cost many their jobs, friends or family. It takes strength, not weakness, to walk in integrity, holiness, and righteousness. Someone usually gets hurt. It takes strength to do right in God's eyes. Just because someone does you wrong, do not let it blind you to what's right according to God, even with covenant relationships!

Hosea 10:12 reads, "Sow for yourselves righteousness; Reap in mercy; Break up your fallow ground, For *it is* time to seek the Lord, Till He comes and rains righteousness on you." You cannot keep sowing into the "unrighteous" kingdom of darkness and expect a "righteous" crop from the kingdom of God. To follow the paths of God, your flesh has to be subjected to the Spirit of God!

What are you sowing into your covenant relationships? Galatians 6:7-8 reads, "Do not be deceived, God is not mocked; for whatever a man sows, that he will also reap. For he who sows to his flesh will of the flesh reap corruption, but he who sows to the Spirit will of the Spirit reap everlasting life." Many relationships reaped corruption because they allowed the flesh to rule, leading them away from righteousness into the unrighteousness, to break up covenant relationships. Every action, thought, or decision has consequences that can trigger reactions.

I had my share of watching broken covenants take place in many relationships. I saw it as a child growing up among family. I saw family and friends have affairs while married. I had pacts with friends that were broken. As a teenager, a best friend accused me of stealing and sleeping with her boyfriend in High School. He had already isolated her from her family and soon isolated her from her friends. He was seeing someone, but it was not me. She confronted me and showed off in front of a large crowd. I was not saved then, so I won't repeat what I said. At that time, I didn't want someone who had children. I was a teenager with my own concerns; I wanted to enjoy what time I could from turmoil. They had a child already and another one on the way. I never would have considered him. By the time she found out the truth, our friendship was finished. She thought we would go back to being friends. Although I forgave her, I never wanted to resume a covenant friendship with her again. But I truly didn't know what a covenant relationship meant at that age, but I found out as an adult.

I was a happy bride who waited a long time to marry the man of God, who became my husband. Over the years, I fasted, prayed, and started walking holy; this was many, many years before he came into the picture. I wasn't sleeping around or living a lifestyle of fornication. At the wedding, when we came to the marriage vows "for better, for worse," I had no idea the "worst" that I would encounter.

I listened to them give us prophecies at our wedding and wondered what was going to take place in my marriage. I remember my maid of honor, who understood the Prophetic, helping me to get ready to leave the church. She said, "I don't know what's going to happen, but remember the words of those prophecies. You two will come through it." Because I was in wedding mode, I could not come back to really listen to the prophecies again, until after the honeymoon. When I typed each of those prophecies out later, I just shook my head, cried, and knew I would have to always remain prayerful.

It was years before I actually learned the verbal truth about the broken covenant. It involved infidelity and a child outside the marriage. It can take you to a place of devastation in your mind. The devastation from this broken covenant left me with great grief. I questioned my purpose, my identity as a wife, mother, minister, and Prophetess. I lost my will, desires in life, and self-esteem. I didn't want to be around anyone because I felt everyone knew but me; I thought I was the laughing stock of the area. It was a small area, and many did know about it.

It was hard to hold my head up high and be joyful. How could I? My life was devastated. It was humiliating, shameful, and caused much internal pain. It was a pain I was sure I'd never be able to escape. Many can tell you what they would do if they were in your shoes, sometimes to the point of being very judgmental. No one truly knows what they will do in the place of another, due to broken covenant, unless they have actually walked the paths and conditions that person walked.

Many spouses truly know when something is not right; that their mate has broken the marriage covenant. Those with a strong sense of discernment know instantly, even if the spouse never says anything about it or tries to deny it. They know . . . because the person may begin to change and do things out of the ordinary, they know because of the calls that come in from the intruder to let the spouse know they are around. They know when you begin to please the lover, and the spouse is lacking. Really, it should cause everyone to look at themselves. Most spouses sometimes feel it was their fault. It's really sad when all parties are confessing Christians. There is no way we can truly satisfy a person of God when we operate with a deceitful, cheating heart.

What do you do when the marriage has not been honored by all, or the marriage bed has not been kept pure, or individuals have not remained faithful? Even if the cheating spouse never says anything, it's possible for their mate to find out when others are brought into the relationship to defile the marriage bed. Hebrew 13:4 reads, "Marriage is honorable among all, and the bed undefiled; but fornicators and adulterers God will judge." The enemy always has a set time to expose. This is happening more among believers in Christ! Many attend church, but don't let God control their life or actions. We don't have to be empowered by Satan to let him use us as a pawn for "his purpose." We can always allow God to arise within us and force the enemy of our soul to flee. We have the power within us to choose the path of life or the path to death.

In the case of adultery, people can continue affairs and affect the lives of those around them. When there is a lack of discretion or accountability in covenant relations, more can be transferable than spirits, brokenness, and soul ties. Soul ties leave you tied to those individuals. Broken covenants can cause and transfer hurts, betrayal, embarrassment, shame, ridicule, lack of trust or confidence, STDs/STIs, and yes, even children born outside the marriage. There's always a cost for all involved. It could cause the breakup of a marriage. It may even cause a fruit of closeness or distance, with outside children. Growing up, I witnessed many outside children who never got a chance to know their fathers or their father's families. Many were hurt and wanted the love of their fathers also. There were others who got used to them not being around and stopped caring.

I've seen cheating men protective of their daughters, moms, or sisters, and I've seen cheating women protective of their sons, fathers, or brothers. They would never consider mistreating them. Yet, some of these same men and women wouldn't give a second thought about destroying someone else's daughter or son they are in a marriage with. If you're not faithful to God and your flesh rules your life, it may be hard to be faithful in your marriage. If you're letting the Holy Spirit guide you, He will always put a check within your spirit to warn you. You just can't ignore the check or warning signals.

As a married woman of God, I'm not friends with males that have to be a secret to my husband. This helps protect me, my marriage, and my husband, and closes doors the enemy could open to infidelity or adultery. It's not that I never encounter temptation; it's just that the Greater One within me *keeps me*. Because He provides the way of escape by listening to the Holy Spirit, sin to commit infidelity does not overpower my life. He doesn't have to force me to choose righteousness. I willingly walked in obedience to God's way and His path of escape for me. What the world has to offer is not worth the cost of me, sinning against God with my body or my heart. So, I choose to close doors that the enemy opens, that would have enticed by the lustfulness of sin. The Greater One has me, and I'm not enticed by what, or who, the enemy tries to use.

Broken covenants in marriages may need deliverance to take place, individually, to walk in total healing from a wounded heart. It can produce fear, secret, or turmoil entrapments that can lead to bondages. God desires that our heart and mind be healed and free. Once you are healed from that type of hurt, you can trust God to keep you and use you to help others.

Running to people or material things to fill those wounds won't help. They cannot replace the peace of God, which surpasses all understanding. They cannot replace walking in integrity, righteousness, holiness, or faithfulness. When the heart and mind have been through much turmoil due to a broken covenant, our hearts and minds must be guarded through Christ Jesus.

We don't have to be fooled by the enemy to break covenant relationships. We can choose to walk in the discernment of God and live a life of righteousness, which does not have to be a struggle. We must let Christ rule in our hearts to fulfill His plans and purposes. Even when people don't serve Him whole heartily, or stay committed to vows made, it does not mean that we have to do the same. Just because they didn't value you or the relationship enough to walk away from the enemy's temptations, does not mean we have to do the same.

Don't seek revenge - pray for them, forgive them, and then leave them in the hands of the Lord. Hebrews 10:30-31 reads, "For we know Him who said, "Vengeance is Mine, I will repay," says the Lord. And again, "The Lord will judge His people." It is a fearful thing to fall into the hands of the living God." You don't want revenge to cause you to be in trouble with the Lord. Don't let bitterness consume you because your marriage endured much pain and hurt by those close who betrayed you.

Broken covenants may make things appear dark around you and your peace missing, but it was prophesied in Luke 1:79 that Jesus would come, "To give light to those who sit in darkness and the shadow of death, To guide our feet into the way of peace." It takes God's peace, guiding you in the midst of this worst storm in your life, but it's a job He can handle well. It also takes walking in forgiveness toward all individuals involved, even if they never, ever acknowledge their wrongdoing. They may not want to walk in God's light, but don't let this stop you from walking in it.

Remember, broken covenants cannot stop the purpose and plan God desires to do through and for you. It cannot stop His favor on your life that God desires others to see. It can push you higher into destiny, even when the enemy thought it was going to kill you. Many lives can be affected positively by your example of love, faithfulness, and freedom in God and with others. With God, we never have to stay in captivity, because healing is always possible, even among broken covenants.

War for Your Marriage

> "And they overcame him by the blood of the Lamb and by the word of their testimony, and they did not love their lives to the death."
> -Revelation 12:11 (AMP)

One of the biggest and most enduring areas that I have ever had to war over in prayer has been my marriage. What I have learned is that as we endeavor to overcome the enemy of our souls, we cannot truly help others if we continue to be superficial concerning the things we encounter in life or our personal testimonies.

One thing I do know is that God-inspired prayers work and can change lives and situations. It does not matter that resistance happens to stop us from interceding; many times, it makes us aware of the spiritual warfare that has come against us. We don't ever have to back away from the resistance, because "He who is in us is greater than he who is in the world." The Greater One lives inside of us, and He shows us how to fight back through intercession.

Although my marriage might have appeared or seemed like everything was okay from the outside, there were times that, on the inside, it was a different story. Psalm 37:4 says, "Delight yourself also in the Lord, And He shall give you the desires of your heart."

I've always spent much time delighting myself in the Lord. Even before I ever married, my heart's desire for my marriage was that we would both operate in the Fruit and Gifts of the Holy Spirit, fulfilling His purpose; and that our marriage would manifest the Glory of God so that HE would get the glory and praise!

Obviously, when looking at many Christian's marriages, it seems like the enemy has been doing a successful job of keeping couples from manifesting the Fruit and Gifts of the Holy Spirit together so that they will not be a threat to his kingdom. He has them looking at faults, instead of the Power of God, so that they will not be effective in tearing down the kingdom of darkness together.

When the demonic enemies cause circumstances to take place; like adultery, children produced outside the marriage and interferences of people entering into the relationship; it can be followed by much pain and shame. It can cause some spouses to be defeated in their hearts, with their commitment toward each other when they look at the faults instead of the principalities, the powers, the rulers of darkness, or the spiritual hosts of wickedness causing the divisions between them.

Sometimes divorce can seem like an easy solution to take when you have given up on your marriage. With the divorce rate as high in the church as in the world, it takes much work, prayer, commitment, and sometimes emotional healing to make the marriages work.

I know we did not always stand *together*, and war over our marriage, and the enemy was allowed to enter, having the upper hand in some areas. As we approached our twentieth anniversary, the attacks became so severe, and with such intensity, that they caused us both to want to walk away and give up on the marriage. I always had a sense that a broken covenant took place years earlier, in some way, but was hidden from me while waiting for the opportune time to do the most damage. The Scripture is true in Mark 4:22 (NIV), where it reads, "For whatever is hidden is meant to be disclosed, and whatever is concealed is meant to be brought out into the open." I just didn't know how true it would be for me.

What should have been a happy, joyful occasion was anything but happy. Therefore, we did not know if we would even make it to our twentieth year. Over the years, I've seen mostly "church folk" gossip about the breakup of marriages, instead of praying for or over them. When it hit me, I found it hard to pray, stand, believe, or move forward in the beginning! I was angry, wounded, hurt, defeated, discouraged, wanted to give up, and ashamed to be in, what I thought was supposed to be a Godly marriage, BUT GOD! It was time to use what I have learned and war in prayer!

When you hear the voice of God as a Prophetic person, you learn very quickly that He will not leave you in that negative state of mind when you are submitted TO Him and have submitted ALL to Him! If you allow God, He will always provide the way for you to walk into His healing.

When you have to minister to others, He never wants you to stand there and bleed on His people! You can use all of that negative stuff that comes against you to help someone else. I can remember being ordained in Georgia and the prophet saying, "You will teach FROM your hurt, and NOT IN your hurt! From your hurt, you will HELP many people! But when people teach IN their hurt, they will hurt others!" I never want to be the person that teaches IN their hurts! Although I knew hurt, I really never fully understood what that prophecy clearly would mean to me. One day, I found out! I stood, teaching with a smile on my face, with so much pain in my heart that it felt like a knife was in it, flowing with the Holy Spirit and speaking the oracles of God, without bleeding on His people.

I felt like Leah, so unloved at the time by my husband, that I had to meditate on many Scriptures, especially Isaiah 54:5 over and over, which read, "For your Maker is your husband, The Lord of hosts is His name; And your Redeemer is the Holy One of Israel; He is called the God of the whole earth." During the years, God has spoken many words as I walked out my deliverance and healing in many areas. Many of the words He gave me were not just for me. Someone reading this, right now, might need to hear the same prophetic encouragement that He gave me in the following:

Be not dismayed! You're not responsible for the doors he allowed to be opened to the enemy. You're responsible for the ones you allowed to be open to the enemy. Whether it be you or him, the choice to make good or bad decisions rests with you both! Choices have consequences! 'Sin may be sweet at first, but later, its consequences bring despair.'

You choose the decisions, but you don't get to choose the consequences! And yes, sometimes innocent parties get hurt. But I deal with all parties, and all parties will have to answer to Me! I don't need you to ever get revenge or do wrong because wrong was done to you! "Vengeance is mine, I will repay!" Therefore, let go of the anger and the hurt! Choose to walk in forgiveness!

There's a call on your life! I called you! No matter how you feel right now, don't let this separate you from Me! You have to stand for righteousness and stand in integrity, even when your spouse won't! You don't have to dummy down to be on someone else's level when they are not at the level that I want them to be! Be who you are in Christ! Only what YOU do for Christ will last!

Have you forgotten that you do have spiritual authority and the power to change your atmosphere? Yes, you may feel broken, and the pain may be deep, but the broken become masters at what they mastered! You will master this! Let not your heart be trouble! Whatever troubles you, troubles Me! Whatever comes against you, comes against Me, because you are Mine!

My chosen vessel! You confessed Me as your Lord! I AM close to those who have a broken heart, who are discouraged and have given up hope, who have suffered disappointments and are crushed in their spirit. I AM close to you right now!

Nothing is too hard, too difficult, or impossible with Me! Instead of your shame, you shall have double honor, and instead of confusion, you shall rejoice in your portion! I know you don't feel like rejoicing now, but keep moving forward in faith, no matter how hard the challenge or sacrifice! You're still a blessed child of Mines! Renew your strength now, because I AM your strength!

Through many stages of the storms of life, God has always spoken and given me prayer strategies in areas, even when I wasn't very strong in Him and in prayer! When the enemy tried continuously to bring defeat, I had to get to the place where I declared, "Enough is enough, no more defeat!" It was time to war with specific prayer strategies, given by God to pray, even in times of extreme warfare.

I didn't pray inappropriately because I have a "blood-bought right" to fight for my marriage, my children, my family, and everything God entrusted to me! I did see victories with the strategies He gave, in many areas. Each of us might have different paths to take, but God taught me to war according to the circumstances and situations I encountered in life. Many people have encountered similar situations.

As God trains your hands for war and your fingers for battle, He will also give you the words to decree and declare for your particular situation. Death and life are in the power of the tongue, and God can give you specific warring strategies to pray personally over your life, your spouse, your children, your family, and all that pertains to you.

In learning this, I pled the Blood of Jesus and spoke DEATH AGAINST what came against our marriage; and spoke LIFE ON what was to be protected by God! I sought HIM for the way to war, the solutions, and the prayer strategies to declare. There are prayer points in the Appendix II section, inspired by God, to help you war over in prayer! They're long and broken out into sections, but then again, they are MARRIAGE WARRING PRAYERS!

If you're not married, change them to whatever promise or situation God has declared you should war over; and then war in prayer over your situation!

When the Losses are Deep

I *don't know which loss* is greater — the loss of identity, a parent, a sibling, a marriage, or a career. One of the hardest things to experience is a series of spiritual warfare attacks during those times when losses are deep. There's nothing worse than going through a process of grief to discover that you are, or feel, all alone.

Spiritual warfare does not take a break just because we experience a loss. If we're not careful, the enemy will use negative thinking to battle us within our minds. The Helmet of Salvation is always needed to protect our mind during times of loss. I would need to protect not only my mind, but also my heart for every loss I encounter.

This was the most difficult chapter to write because the void and pain from the loss of my mom were still deep in my heart. Even as I write, I miss the woman of God that He allowed to birth me. I'll always be thankful and grateful to Him for placing me within her womb. I started and stopped this chapter so many times, before and after her death. When I picked it back up to complete, it was my first Mother's Day without her; I had to adjust to new feelings and let the emotions flow. So, I asked God, "Where do I begin, Lord, with this chapter?" His response was, "Where you are now is a good place to start."

In the fall of 2018, Mom's health really took a turn, and she called me, crying. I had noticed changes over the years with her, during the loss of many that were close to her. The signs of her declining health had started years before, after the death of my stepdad, and it seemed to get worse after my brother and her five brothers' deaths. Those close to her knew instantly that something was not right; that she had become depressed and somewhat forgetful. Those who were not close could only say that I was exaggerating or making something out of nothing. But that was my mother; they didn't know her as I knew her. With those seven deaths, she became more depressed, but my brother's death really sent her spiraling downward into a deeper depression.

I wanted her to move, years earlier, to be close because she was in Tennessee, and I was in Alabama. Mom fought moving, and many times would pretend everything was okay, so I wouldn't worry. When she called me that day, I left, headed for Tennessee. The moment I saw her, I knew instantly I had to step in as her POA (Power of Attorney). She didn't fight this time. I made an appointment at her doctor's office because she had lost so much weight and was very confused. Her personal business was not taken care of, and she was double dosing on medication she should not have been taking. Her memory had definitely been affected over the years. I won't write everything that happened, but I knew she could no longer live alone.

As I prepared her home to put on the market, Mom became sicker. If I could have just been able to deal with her sickness, maybe it would have helped me some. Instead, I encountered spiritual warfare from every angle in my life. I didn't know what to focus on, due to the attacks on every side. I needed my mom, but she was steadily declining and could not help me now. I prayed, fasted, and asked

God for a clearer focus and clarity on what to do. I felt persecuted for wanting to take care of her; there was nothing else to do, except keep seeking God until His answer came. He made it quite clear that I needed to focus on my mom because I wouldn't have as much time as I thought I needed. I was devastated because I wasn't ready for her to go.

In my relationship with the Lord, I was communing and praying to Him daily. It didn't take a forty-day fast to see what He wanted me to do. I heard His voice clearly and am so thankful that I listened and obeyed Him. In the NIV, 1 Timothy 5:4 reads, "But if a widow has children or grandchildren, these should learn first of all to put their religion into practice by caring for their own family and so repaying their parents and grandparents, for this is pleasing to God." How could I stand as a minister or a woman of God, and not minister to her needs because someone didn't want me to? My mom was a widow who was definitely in need, and I was not going to act like she didn't exist.

When you allow God's Word to be a light to your path and you meditate on His truths, your way becomes clear on what you have to do. I honored my mom and did what was required of me as her only living child. I requested a chest X-ray because she had this nagging cough that had existed too long; plus, her weight had dropped to about one hundred thirty pounds and continued to drop to under one hundred pounds. The nurse was trying to say that it was her high blood pressure medication, but I sensed in my spirit that was not right and wanted her checked out before moving her. Mom was diagnosed with stage four lung cancer, and I had less than nine months with her, although I didn't know it at the time. Had I not stepped in when I did and moved her, I believe I would have lost my mom sooner, without being there or ever knowing she was sick with cancer.

After the shock of her diagnosis, the tears flowed many days and nights. Even after the move, I often went into the closet above her room downstairs and decreed and declared prayers over her until I fell asleep, prostrate on the floor. At times, I slept on the couch near her room when she wasn't feeling well so that I could quickly be there when she needed me, because she was coughing and choking on bloody mucus. I changed and dressed wounds that did not heal. In the end, it was painful for anyone to touch, bathe, and lift her. She just screamed and cried, "Please, Mom... don't." She thought I was her mother. This really stabbed me in the heart because I was as gentle as I could possibly be.

She also screamed and cried with the CNA (Certified Nurse Assistant) and nurses, until finally, hospice told me, "You're going to have to let her take something to calm her down." I knew what that meant, and it only caused my heart to hurt worse. I went upstairs where she couldn't hear and cried my heart out. She showed every sign that she was getting ready to leave.

I prayed that God would give her a restful sleep. He answered those prayers many times over, before her death. Mom later told a church member that I didn't just start taking care of her because she was sick. I had taken care of her and my brother ever since I was a child. She didn't want me to take care of her in her sickness because of all of the work, but I wanted her to still feel my love as she exited out of this world and into eternity.

I knew Mom was holding on until she knew I was okay with her leaving. Maybe she felt that I would attempt to leave with her by suicide. I found it hard, so very hard to let go, but I did. I was with my mom until the very end, saying to her, "Mom, it is all right, Mama. It is okay. I know you're tired. If you're ready to see Jesus, I'll be fine. I'll never do anything to disgrace you or God. I'm so glad God placed me in your womb. You were a good mother to Jimmy and me. And if you are ready to go, it's alright. I'll be fine; we'll all be fine. It's okay." The rest of the night, while she made small noises, I kept saying, "It's okay, it's okay! I'm here." My mom was gone less than three hours later.

My brother's death was another loss that struck me deep within the heart. He seemed to just struggle throughout life, not quite finding his place, sometimes through homelessness. He stayed on the West Coast in California, moving back toward Indiana, only occasionally. He never stayed long in one place because of the restlessness within him.

When I moved out of the house, he had decided to go into the Navy. Not sure what happened to him there, but he was never the same coming out. Sometimes it seemed like he and Mom were like water and oil; the two did not mix well. I know it was from the years of hurt that he never dealt with from our childhood. There were times that I could protect him, and there were times that I could not. I told Mom how I wished his life would have taken a different path. Her response was, "You were the one who raised him." She made it seem like it was my fault that he had turned out the way he did. All this was before we dealt with our own set of issues. I took those remarks about him personally. For years, I thought it was my fault that his life took a bad turn.

I could no more help him than I could myself at the time. We both were drowning in unresolved hurt, and I was also raising my daughter. He told me that he felt forsaken by me, just as much as he felt it by our parents. We tried to help him many times. We could only help, just a little, before anger took control over him. He was like a ticking bomb waiting to explode; he developed the thought that I had it better in life than him.

We grew up in the same home, encountered the same treatment, but he saw me as the favorite child. For so many years, it was just us, so I always tried to protect him when we were kids. I could not protect him as an adult. Our relationship suffered, and I lost the connection with my baby brother.

For many years, we only heard from him when he was in trouble or needed help. During the years of silence, he was badly beaten by policemen. When they called from the hospital, and we could talk to him, his voice was never the same. Mom tried to help him get back on his feet many times. She brought him to Tennessee to live with her and my stepdad, from time to time. My brother remained a troubled man and did well until he wanted her to pay for his childhood hurts. It was hatred that she could not keep enduring because it caused problems in her home.

When he went back to California, he got so bad that he was rushed to the hospital, and we almost lost him. Mom had to fly out to California to be with him. He was homeless with no place to go, but her plans were to bring him back to Tennessee. After he was released, they stayed at a hotel across the street from the VA hospital while he was recovering.

The hatred resumed from childhood; he wanted to kill my mom. We could not get in touch with her because he had her cell phone. He would not let her answer the hotel phone. I never heard my Mom talk in a fearful way like that when we were able to reach her. When we found out what had happened, we told her to go to the manager if he left the room. We were already making arrangements for her to leave. She went to a different room, and the manager told the staff not to mention where she was moved if my brother asked.

My daughter made arrangements for her to fly out the very next day. This was her baby, so she didn't want to leave him like that. Her motherly heart still left food and money at the desk for him. But she decided that he would have to seek help before she could help him again. Proverb 4:23 says, "Keep your heart with all diligence, For out of it *spring* the issues of life." My brother developed heart problems; we always believed it stemmed from issues he had not dealt with in his heart. We saw him live three good years, it seemed, with peace. We were able to talk to him and keep in contact. He had his very first place and was doing well until that restlessness took over his life again. The restlessness and the hatred returned toward Mom and me. We lost my brother way before he had actually died.

In December 2014, he passed away at the age of fifty-two. He never really accomplished some of the things that he desired, and he never resolved some of his issues. He was angry at life, and we found out later that he always wished he was dead. He died from pulmonary artery aneurysms. The hospital found my number in his items and contacted me fifteen minutes before he passed. I believe I handled his death worse than my mom's death because of unresolved issues in his life.

I encountered many other deep losses that included my career, betrayal by those close to me, and a loss of identity. With each of these losses, the spiritual warfare was intense every step of the way. It was intense before and during the caring for my mom, her funeral, with my brother's relationship and his funeral, the loss of my career, and even with people I trusted.

Due to the attacks, I allowed myself to enter into a level of grief that was trying to take me back into bondage. We can't always blame others when we allow ourselves to be captured in bondage to the enemy plan. God made it clear to my inner man that it was a danger to let anyone have that much power over my life. That power should have never been taken out of God's hands and placed into the hands of others. I had to retake the power and the authority Christ gave me back from the enemy.

We all will experience losses in life that are deep and dear to our hearts. When I wrote this chapter, the Coronavirus (COVID-19) was taking lives all across the world, affecting many nations. I like the AMPC version of John 16:33; it reads, "I have told you these things, so that in Me you may have [perfect] peace and confidence. In the world you have tribulation and trials and distress and frustration; but be of good cheer [take courage; be confident, certain, undaunted]! For I have overcome the world. [I have deprived it of power to harm you and have conquered it for you.]." When losses are deep, the enemy always overplays his hand with God. Losses, trials, distress, and frustration will happen in life, but we don't have to let it conquer us to the point of giving up hope.

Many times, it may take you, fighting as if your life depended on it. God has promised to never leave us or forsake us. He has given us many Scriptures to meditate on while coping and healing from our losses. Lean on your supporters during those difficult times. It's not the time to reflect on who you thought should have been there.

God has people specifically assigned to give you words of encouragement. Don't you give up! Look up to the Author and Finisher of our Faith! He will never leave you comfortless. You have the Holy Spirit for that!

The Ability to Dream Again

"The prophet who has a dream, let him tell a dream; And he
who has My word, let him speak My word faithfully."
-Jeremiah 23:28

W hat do you do when it seems like your dreams have died, and
you've lost your ability to dream again? You may have lost it
due to some trials, challenges, or even setbacks. The enemy always
uses a battlefield of the mind to stop a dream from being fulfilled.
I'm not talking about the dreams that we have when we fall asleep,
but the dreams or desires God placed in our hearts to succeed in life.

There were many attempts to stop this book from being written.
But it was a dream God placed within my heart to birth forth, many
years ago. Sometimes it was through situations or people designed
to crush my spirit, causing me to give up hope. On the battlefield
of my mind, I heard, "No one wants to hear your story! It's too late!
You're too old to be used! You can't help anyone!" What the enemy
was saying, through thoughts, people, and circumstances, was that
my life had no purpose and that I was not valued.

Perhaps you may have similar feelings like that. God wants you to
know that your validation is found in Him, not them. He values you
and created you for purpose! When I had those feelings, He allowed
me to hear encouraging words in my mom's voice. I believe the words

will also encourage you to fulfill whatever the Lord has told you to do. The words were:

"Write that book, baby, and crush the head of the enemy with your praise! Speak on what life has taught you! The Greater One lives within you to help you! You are not powerless! Take back, from the enemy's hand, the power God gave you! Pick up your dreams and live again! Every negative thing happening to you, give it to the Lord!

Don't you stop praising God because someone doesn't see your value! God has always valued you, in and out of the turmoil of life, from the very beginning! If they never do anything else for you, God still will!

Don't let your gifts die within you due to attacks from the enemy, by those who don't know they're being used by him! You are a child of a King, in relationship with the Lord! Now walk like it with your head held high, not downcast, and do whatever God tells you to do!"

Then the Lord spoke to my spirit, "MY PLANS for you will be fulfilled! You are covered under MY CARE and MY WILL!" When God brings you out of wilderness or desert places, not only do you come out equipped and strengthened, but you come out empowered with the Holy Spirit!

I couldn't regain my ability to pick up my dreams again until I overcame my fears. There were fears with abandonment issues, deep-rooted shame, facing truths about relationships with mother, spouse, and others — what they thought, not letting my voice be heard due to failure, hurts, judgments, oppression, pain, rejection, and spiritual warfare. Many times, I didn't allow the gifting God placed within me to come forth because of some of these fears. I would dummy down my ministry gifts, sometimes to intimidation to suit others.

This left me feeling defeated and frustrated in my Christian walk until God's power arises within me. Psalm 68:1 says, "Let God arise, Let His enemies be scattered." God, begin to scatter the enemies from my mind, heart, and life! I could no longer drown in anger, fear, or shame for allowing myself to be in some hard situations that took life away from me. I was not going to just lie down and die when there were purposes still to be fulfilled in my life. I found solace in the Word of God, walked in forgiveness, released others, and got delivered. Freedom continued in the ability to praise the Lord in dance through the storms. As freedom took over my heart, I saw the enemy lose a foothold over my life, with praise. I praised the Lord during situations when the enemy was trying to keep me in captivity. I knew I was supposed to soar as an eagle, but I was not soaring.

Being in captivity reminded me of an eagle I saw at an Amusement Park Zoo in Pennsylvania. The bird was the most depressing eagle, and it reminded me of depressed people who are injured by others. I can remember getting angry and saying that the eagle should not be in captivity; they should release it. I didn't know that eagles, in captivity, can no longer survive the wild when they have been injured by human activities.

Many people are injured by others to where they no longer feel they can survive in life. The enemy loves to take us into captivity, like that eagle, to keep us from soaring with God. I came out of captivity, regained my strength, and regained my voice to be heard because I had something to say. My book would be written. Anytime you're not ready to face the truth about your issues, you're not ready to be delivered and healed. Many sit in churches, ministry positions, and in the pulpit, not healed and bleeding on the people. God's Word is truth, and He wants us to call on Him in truth. When we know the truth, we can be set free by it.

The longer you stay unhealed, you can lose your ability to fulfill your God-ordained dreams and purposes. Now, I didn't say you wouldn't fulfill yours, but if our dreams or plans are not in alignment with God's plans and purposes, they go unfulfilled. When plans, purposes, and dreams are given by the Lord, He knows the "plans to prosper you and not to harm you, plans to give you hope and a future." God desires you to have those dreams come forth – the ones He has placed within you. We are living in the days when God is doing just like Acts 2:17-18 said:

> "And it shall come to pass in the last days, says God, That I will pour out of My Spirit on all flesh; Your sons and your daughters shall prophesy, Your young men shall see visions, Your old men shall dream dreams. And on My menservants and on My maidservants I will pour out My Spirit in those days; And they shall prophesy."

God is pouring out His Spirit on us, to see visions and dreams He has placed in our hearts, which will carry over to future generations. Many gifts and dreams lay dormant in people because they are snatched by the enemy. What is the enemy trying to steal, kill, and destroy in your life to prevent purpose or your dreams from being fulfilled? What is in your hand that God wants you to use to bless others? Perhaps, behind your biggest struggle, or trial, lay the solutions to your dreams.

Throughout my life, I discovered creativity that I didn't know I possessed, until challenges came along. Some were used on the job, and others were used in ministry. I had no idea what, or how to begin many projects, but I knew the One who did. Solutions were given whenever I did what Proverb 3:5-6 states, "Trust in the Lord with all your heart, And lean not on your own understanding; In all your ways acknowledge Him, And He shall direct your paths."

I was more surprised when the assigned projects were completed than the people that assigned them. I had to trust this Scripture a lot with my mom and continue to for any challenge. She was always getting me to head something up, like I knew what I was doing. She kept me in constant prayer by putting me on the spot. She often told people, "Don't worry. Rita got it. She'll take care of it." Most times, I was thinking, "She'll take care of what? What're you getting me into now?"

I've had pastors that would do the same . . . put people on the spot. I guess they were making sure we were ready, in and out of season. With all of the challenging assignments given to me, it helped me to get ready to birth forth dreams that God placed within me.

So, what creativity in dreams have you buried within that the Lord wants you to release? I'm amazed at the creativity many have that don't think they have anything to offer. Life has blinded them to the blessings in their hands to generate future income or businesses. I want to encourage you to not back away from what God wants you to do. He holds not only the plans, but also the strategies and the solutions for you to succeed with your dreams. He may even remove people from your paths that are not destined to be a part of your future. When it's time to build in your life, God may not leave the ones around who constantly tear you down.

Some never fulfill their dreams or purposes because they allow fear or people to pull them down to their level. When God is taking you to your next level, not everybody will be able to go with you. They may not be ready to be challenged or transformed to do the work of the Lord.

Unfortunately, many people are satisfied not to be used by Him, so they never fulfill what He placed in them. They may even try to keep you from yours. You cannot afford to let people stop you from fulfilling a dream the Lord gave to you. People who lean on their own understanding, instead of the Lord's, may try to stop you with man's wisdom instead of Godly wisdom. But what did God tell you to do?

There may come a time in your life when you have to push past the fear, turmoil, and obstacles, even if they are people. There may be a time, like in the Scriptures, that God "takes hold of your right hand and says to you, Do not fear; I will help you." As God leads you, He may have you make decisions that you didn't think you could. His purpose is for His Will to be fulfilled in your life. Your purpose is to do it. You have the ability to dream again and birth them forth, and you can do this with God's help.

Conclusion

> "Have you not known? Have you not heard? The everlasting God, the LORD, The Creator of the ends of the earth, Neither faints nor is weary. His understanding is unsearchable. He gives power to the weak, And to *those who have* no might He increases strength. Even the youths shall faint and be weary, And the young men shall utterly fall, But those who wait on the LORD Shall renew *their* strength; They shall mount up with wings like eagles, They shall run and not be weary, They shall walk and not faint." -Isaiah 40:28-31

W*hen we began this* journey together, I shared an eagle story with you in the introduction. I would like to end it with another eagle story. During the worst time of my life, when I wanted to give up, I was driving home alone. I had worked the night shift, and the next morning attended classes at Purdue University. I was tired, both physically and spiritually. The physical condition I knew would be taken care of with a little rest, but the spiritual condition I knew God would have to handle and help me through. It was then that He spoke to my spirit, to look to the sky.

When I looked up, I saw an eagle, soaring in a circle way above my car. The eagle went wherever I drove. As I turned, the eagle turned also; I ended up pulling over to the side of the road to watch it. It still circled above me. It looked huge while closer, but as it soared higher and higher, the size seemed smaller. I watched that eagle until I lost sight of it, thinking that I was seeing things. God, then, began to minister to me right there in the car. He made it clear that, just as that eagle was soaring high above me, He was going to have me soar above much of the turmoil the enemy had used against me to keep me in spiritual bondage. God made it clear that I was in the process of being rejuvenated for better purposes, according to His plans. Although I felt alone, He had me notice the eagle was flying alone to higher heights.

I, too, would need to release things and people that were keeping me from acceleration and accomplishing things His way, sometimes alone. Although I hated some of the storms I encountered in life, He made it clear that the eagles use their strength to help them reach greater heights. All of the storms, obstacles, challenges, frustrations, and turmoil were used to push me toward the fulfillment of destiny, as long as I remain focused, just like the eagle. He made it clear that although He was training me, there would come a time that I would train others to soar above their life's turmoil, also.

I was truly encouraged before finishing that drive home. At the time, I lived in Gary, Indiana, and I never heard of eagles in that area. That night, when I went to work, I shared with a co-worker that I thought I had seen an eagle, but was scared to mention it. Another co-worker who was listening said that there had been reports of an eagle in that area, and I probably did see it. I had always felt that the eagle was put there by God, to save my life and to encourage me to move forward.

Many of the chapters in this book began with questions. They were put there for reflection and to show that you're not alone when facing the turmoil of life. They're questions that can be presented to the Lord for any situation concerning our life.

1 Peter 4:8 reads, "And above all things have fervent love for one another, for 'love will cover a multitude of sins.'" Love covers a multitude of sins, but that doesn't mean it covers all sins. It does not hide the sins the Lord desires to deal with in our lives. It does not cover the things that cause us to self-destruct and bring hurt to others. That's why deliverance is necessary and helpful for people to obtain freedom in Christ. They must be dealt with in whatever way, or setting, God leads you.

Each of the chapters could have been a book in itself. The worst parts of what happened in my life were not included in this book. My goal is not to continue a cycle of hurt, leaving people defeated, but of deliverance and freedom in order to help others. Many hurts and turmoil were dealt with at the appropriate times, with the appropriate people and in the appropriate settings.

God desires to deal with the issues of our hearts so that we can experience freedom in Christ. That's why we are told in Galatians 5:1 to "Stand fast, therefore, in the liberty by which Christ has made us free, and do not be entangled again with a yoke of bondage." The enemy uses many scenarios to try to keep our mind in bondage, so we never accomplish the plans and purpose God desires us to do.

We're told in Scripture that there is a time to be silent and a time to speak. God can use those times of silence to heal us from the turmoil that really tried to kill us. In those times of healing, damage from as far back as childhood can be repaired. Many may have had great childhoods, but the turmoil came in their adult years. Whatever way it entered, God can take care of it because nothing is impossible with Him. When you walk in healing and the time comes to speak, He won't allow you to bleed on the people when speaking truth. That is what this book is about.

You may have suffered injustice or were treated badly by those close to you, but Ecclesiastes 3:15 (AMPC) says, "That which is now already has been, and that which is to be already has been; and God seeks that which has passed by [so that history repeats itself]." We can't go back and change the past, but we can change how we will respond to our future. God is right there, within you, ready to help.

Maybe turmoil caused you to lose your identity. God wants to remind you that He took care of that in the very first book of the Bible. Genesis 1:27 says, "So God created mankind in his *own* image, in the image of God He created them; male and female He created them." Your identity is in the image of God, and no person, trial, injustice, or situation can change that.

Perhaps your past of un-holiness caused you to do foolish things and left you feeling weak. God can still use you because we're told in 1 Corinthians 1:27, "But God has chosen the foolish things of the world to put to shame the wise, and God has chosen the weak things of the world to put to shame the things which are mighty . . ."

Perhaps you may not have experienced the love of a father or mother, or they just were not there for you. God has even taken care of that. It reads in Psalm 27:10, "When my father and my mother forsake me, Then the Lord will take care of me." God adopted you as His child before you came into this world, and He is there to take care of your needs.

You may have received unexpected blessings from people and many places. God was using them to gift you with the blessings from Him. James 1:17 says, "Every good and perfect gift is from above, coming down from the Father of the heavenly lights, who does not change like shifting shadows." In fact, God has gifts within you that He desires to come out to bless someone else. So, break open the box that the enemy has tried to keep them in and let them flow to bless others.

There may come a time when God instructs you to move to a different place, from situations or people who can hinder your progress or destiny. He's doing this to fulfill a purpose in your life. It's very important to listen to the instructions that He gives you during those times. You will really have to determine, in your heart, to remain focused on where He leads. Proverb 4:25 says, "Let your eyes look straight ahead, And your eyelids look right before you." With those moves, you may encounter people who don't operate in the path of integrity; they would love to lead you off a path of moral courage, but don't you let them lead you there.

When you're a part of a blended family that is just not blending, there is still reason for their purpose in your life, even if their purpose was to draw you nearer to God so that He could draw nearer to you.

Maybe a covenant was broken among friends and spouses that led you to war in prayer. We are told in the Word to pray without ceasing, even with hard situations in our relationship. You cannot force a person to do what is right. God has given them a free will to choose between those things that are life and death, not only with their words, but also by their actions. They cannot lead you properly when they are not letting the Lord lead them. They cannot even cover you with prayers properly when there's no substance or Word within them. That is why God will sometimes teach you how to war in prayers that are effective and fervent. They have to desire and choose to walk in righteousness in all areas.

Just because they wronged you, don't let it turn you bitter, missing out on what God wants to do through you. He has not left you uncovered just because someone broke a covenant with you. Psalm 34:19 says, "Many are the afflictions of the righteous, But the Lord delivers him out of them all." Even if the people were not truly there for you, God is always there to help us dwell together in unity.

Maybe, in turmoil, you experienced losses of loved ones, jobs, or marriages, and it affected you emotionally, physically, socially, or spiritually. God is close to the broken-hearted, and He saves us when we are crushed in spirit. But in His closeness, He heals the broken-hearted and binds up our wounds.

Don't give up on life, child of God, because of life's turmoil. You have the ability to dream again, in spite of hardship or brokenness. Even with turmoil within us, our hope can still be in the Lord. Many people who come against you, never realized that they are being used by the enemy to deter you from purpose. Don't let this destroy your hope to dream again. Proverb 23:18 (NIV) says, "There is surely a future hope for you, and your hope will not be cut off." Whatever dreams God gave you that you put down, He desires for you to pick them up again and do it!

You may have encountered turmoil, similar to what was shared in this book, or they may be different. Whatever you encounter, God desires you to soar above life's turmoil also. You don't have to do it alone. God has left us with the greatest Helper, our Comforter, our Advocate, our Intercessor, our Counselor, our Strengthener, and our Standby, who is the Holy Spirit representing Christ, acting on His behalf to teach and help us.

Greatness is living within you, because 1 John 4:4 tells us, "He who is in you is greater than he who is in the world." You just need to take back the authority and power that you gave the enemy to use against you. The authority Christ gave the Disciples was for us also, when He said in Luke 10:19, "Behold, I give you the authority to trample on serpents and scorpions, and over all the power of the enemy, and nothing shall by any means hurt you."

When people try to harm you, they're using power from the enemy. Their control over your life, with that misused power, should never be. People with misused power will run to family, friends, new jobs, new marriages, or new relationships, instead of running to God or the Word to deal with their problems. You can always tell where their focus is, or where they're at spiritually, by what comes out of their mouths. You don't have to let this happen to you. Take that power out of the hands of the enemy and leave it where God wants it to be . . . in your hands!

You have a destiny to fulfill that should not be taken to the cemetery. You don't have to dummy down your gift, your talent or whatever God placed in your life to come out to suit others. 1 Peter 4:10 tells us, "As each one has received a gift, minister it to one another, as good stewards of the manifold grace of God." There are souls assigned to your hands to reach in the Kingdom of God.

It's not too late to fulfill purpose when God is telling you to do something. Don't live any more years in fear. Let your voice be fearless in the Kingdom of God. It's time to let your voice be heard. So, soar as an eagle, child of God, and let Him raise you to higher levels in Christ!

30 Daily Empowerment Devotions

As the Lord empowered you through these daily devotions, take time to reflect on His faithfulness through whatever storms may come your way. The devotions were created to help us through the turmoil of life. Sometimes, we're left feeling that no one understands, but God does, and He sees everything you are going through. He sees the good, the bad, and the ugly. His plans for you are good and not evil, plans to give you hope.

So, if you feel like journaling your responses, from the Reflection section, go ahead and do that. If you just want to sit and let the Lord minister to you, do that. If there are concerns within your heart and you think no one wants to hear them, God does, and He wants you to express them. Give it to the Lord in prayer. Seek His face and let His strength replace every weakness that has tried to drown your life away from His presence. Draw your strength from the Lord. You can always rest and believe in His promise that He will never leave you nor forsake you. He's true to His Word, and that's a word He can keep.

So, listen to what the Holy Spirit speaks to your inner man, as you begin your next thirty days of devotion with the Lord!

Day 1

Peace Within

Have you not been feeling strength or peace from God lately? When your peace is affected, make a declaration saying, "I will walk in the peace of God and peace with God!" Don't allow anyone to kill your spirit man by stealing your joy and peace from God. Sadly, sometimes it can come through those so near and dear to your heart.

Don't let this surprise you. Even Jesus was betrayed by someone close to Him – that person was Judas. The Judas' in your life will help push you towards your destiny! Whenever you feel yourself weaken with no strength or peace, draw your strength from the Lord! He shall strengthen your heart!

PRAYER:

Lord, remove all of the unrest and anxieties in my life. Replace them with Your Peace which surpasses all understanding, in Jesus' name I pray, Amen!

REFLECTION: What or who has stolen your joy and peace lately? Ask the Lord to show you how that is pushing you toward or away from destiny. Journal what He tells you.

_____

_____

_____

_____

_____

_____

_____

_____

_____

_____

_____

_____

_____

_____

_____

_____

_____

_____

_____

_____

_____

_____

_____

Day 2

You are not Forsaken

"And the Lord, He is the One who goes before you. He will be with you, He will not leave you nor forsake you; do not fear nor be dismayed."-Deuteronomy 31:8

Have you been thinking that the Lord has forsaken you, and this has caused you much fear? Don't allow yourself to fall into fear or dismay. God has not forgotten about you, and He will never leave you alone. That's a promise we can be sure of. The Lord is right there with you, leading you on His paths of righteousness, according to His Will. All you have to do is follow where He leads!

PRAYER:

Lord, You have not forsaken those who seek You with all their heart. Thank You for taking away the fear of being forsaken and for being a refuge in times of trouble. Father God, let me always feel an awareness of Your presence! In Jesus' name, I pray. Amen!

REFLECTION: What do you do when you can't find your way in the Lord, and you feel all alone? Seek the Lord for ways to help others who may feel the same and journal the different ways you can help.

_____

_____

Day 3

Hidden in Christ

"For you died, and your life is hidden with Christ in God." -Colossians 3:3

Our true identity *"is* hidden with Christ in God." That is why "He must increase, but we must decrease." Hiding behind the greater Glory of our Lord is a great place to be! In the AMPC version of John 3:30, it reads, "He must increase, but I must decrease. [He must grow more prominent; I must grow less so.]."

GROW, GOD, GROW! Let the Lord move and grow into the center of your life; therefore, when people look at you, they will see Christ.

PRAYER:

Father God, always keep my life hidden with Christ so that You will always get the glory. In Jesus' name, I pray. Amen!

REFLECTION: God has placed gifts within you that He is bringing to the front. Journal about how He wants you to use them.

_____

_____

_____

Day 4

Listen to the Lord's Instructions

> "For 'who has known the mind of the Lord that he may instruct Him?' But we have the mind of Christ."
> -1 Corinthians 2:16

As we grow in the Lord, His instructions become clearer when we have the mind of Christ. Jesus was our greatest example to follow. Studying His ways take us from our way of thinking to His way of thinking. There's nothing in life that happens that we cannot use the mind of Christ. It does not matter if it's with turmoil, people, situations, or circumstances; we can always follow his example. I don't know what you are going through in life, but God will take care of you. I don't know what you are thinking, but in your thinking, let it be Christ-like. Even when we don't understand why certain things happen, we can always trust the instructions given by the Lord to develop our mind in Christ!

PRAYER:

Father God, I trust Your instructions and lead. Let me always have the mind of Christ in everything I do or say! In Jesus' name, I pray. Amen!

REFLECTION: As you develop the mind of Christ, do a "negative thought fast," replacing each negative thought with a positive thought for the next thirty days. Whatever negative thought enters into your mind, find a Scripture to replace it that tells you who you are in Christ.

_____

_____

_____

_____

_____

_____

_____

_____

_____

_____

_____

_____

_____

_____

_____

_____

_____

_____

_____

_____

_____

_____

_____

Day 5

Use Your Prophetic Voice

"But he who prophesies speaks edification and exhortation and comfort to men." -1 Corinthians 14:3

Y*ou have a voice* to be used in the kingdom of God! Use your voice to prophesy over your life and others in a godly way. Don't let the enemy shut you down! Don't speak words of death, but life. Prophecy can bring life to you and others that God sends your way. True prophecy speaks edification by building up, uplifting, and strengthening. It speaks exhortation to bring solace, inspires hope, provides encouragement in times of disappointments, or afflictions. It speaks comfort to give consolation, cheers us up, to provide strength and freedom from worry, grief, or distress. Yes, it even speaks times of correction and warning!

Let prophecy show you the treasures in the people, no matter how bad their situation looks. Don't let your words tear people down or beat them up! Are you judging? Let go of it if it was not given to you by God. When people judge with their words, they could be speaking what's in their own hearts! Let the light of the Lord show you what's in your heart. If we never learn the differences of our own weakness, we can be blind to what's in us, assuming to discern something in others that is really a reflection of ourselves. Let's keep our heart right to speak what God says. Then we can speak edification and exhortation and comfort to men.

PRAYER:

Father God, death and life are in the power of the tongue, and I choose to speak life over Your Kingdom. Let me always speak life with words of edification, exhortation, and comfort over your people. In Jesus' name, I pray. Amen!

REFLECTION: How do you hear from God? Do you sense Him speaking through the Holy Spirit? Listen to Him, speak to your spirit, and journal the ways that He wants to use you to speak life to others. Then write out what He tells you for someone today.

_____

_____

_____

_____

_____

_____

_____

_____

_____

_____

_____

_____

_____

_____

_____

Day 6

Don't Compromise Your Relationship with God

"Like a muddied fountain and a polluted spring is a righteous man who yields, falls down, and compromises his integrity before the wicked." -Proverbs 25:26 (AMPC)

When Christian people around you truly love you, they will encourage your relationship with the Lord when they see you falling away. They will honor His anointing in your life and affirm your identity in Christ. You won't have to compromise your principles or relationship with them or Him! What God offers is good and is never designed to harm or damage you! What the wicked offers can bring compromise and pollute your integrity. Don't let it pollute yours!

PRAYER:

Father God, keep my heart and ways on Your paths of righteousness so that I always walk in Your Will. In Jesus' name, I pray. Amen!

REFLECTION: Journal ways that others have kept you from compromising your integrity. Seek the Lord about those around you, now, who could cause you to yield and fall down. Journal what He tells you.

_____

_____

_____

_____

_____

_____

_____

_____

_____

_____

_____

_____

_____

_____

_____

_____

_____

_____

_____

_____

_____

_____

_____

_____

Day 7

Afflictions

"And you became followers of us and of the Lord, having received the word in much affliction, with joy of the Holy Spirit," -1 Thessalonians 1:6

W*hen you receive the* Word in the midst of afflictions, you become an example for others to follow! It does not matter how intense the pressure is — you can still maintain a Christ-like attitude that others would love to imitate. Just make sure that you are following Christ where He leads and that you imitate ALL His ways! When you don't stand for TRUTH, you are liable to stand for anything, including deception! What a trap, lie, and hindrance from the enemy! Determine to walk in, and after the integrity of God, because Psalm 51:6 says, "Behold, You desire truth in the inward parts, And in the hidden part You will make me to know wisdom." Let the Lord keep you walking after truth and righteousness, even when you are persecuted, shunned, or disliked for it!

PRAYER:

Father God, let me always receive Your Word, no matter the affliction life brings, in Jesus' name, I pray. Amen!

REFLECTION: Journal the last affliction that you had with the joy of the Holy Spirit still within you.

_____

_____

_____

_____

_____

_____

_____

_____

_____

_____

_____

_____

_____

_____

_____

_____

_____

_____

_____

_____

_____

_____

_____

_____

Walk in the Spirit

"I say then: Walk in the Spirit, and you shall not fulfill the lust of the flesh." -Galatians 5:16

My *love, never let* anyone cause you to stop displaying the godly Fruit of the Spirit! For it is the Lord who will build your character and motivation to be more like Christ in His kingdom. How are you going to do this? By allowing the work of the Holy Spirit to develop that fruit within you and bring order to your life! Verse 22-23 goes on to say, "But the fruit of the Spirit is love, joy, peace, longsuffering, kindness, goodness, faithfulness, gentleness, self-control." You belong to the Lord, and you CAN walk, and be guided daily by the direction of the Holy Spirit!

PRAYER:

Father God, as the Fruit of the Spirit continues to develop within, bringing order, guide me daily to walk in the Spirit, doing Your will in ways that bring You glory! In Jesus' name, I pray. Amen!

REFLECTION: What's the main fruit the Lord wants you to develop today that you have not displayed and why?

_____

_____

_____

_____

_____

_____

_____

_____

_____

_____

_____

_____

_____

_____

_____

_____

_____

_____

_____

_____

_____

_____

_____

Day 9

Walk Upright

> "Fools mock at sin, But among the upright there is favor."
> -Proverbs 14:9

Whatever *God tells you* to do, DO IT! When God is leading you in one direction, but others want to lead you off that path of righteousness, FOLLOW GOD! His way is best! It's only there that you'll be in special standing and favor with the Lord! Always allow God's integrity to be displayed in your life, so that His favor always follows you!

PRAYER:

Father God, keep me always walking upright because that's where Your favor is! In Jesus' name, I pray. Amen!

REFLECTION: Think and write about an area where you have had a hard time letting God lead you. Why or Why not?

_____

_____

_____

Day 10

On Eagle's Wings

> "But those who wait on the Lord Shall renew their strength; They shall mount up with wings like eagles, They shall run and not be weary, They shall walk and not faint."
> -Isaiah 40:31

When things seem more than you can bear, and you just don't feel the strength to make it through, that's the time to sit on God's wings and allow the current of His wind to carry you far, far above your problems! All you have to do is just trust Him to carry you through. You will regain your strength and the power to keep soaring high like on eagle's wings!

PRAYER:

Father, in the name of Jesus, renew my strength in the Lord. Help me to mount up with wings like eagles. Show me how to run and walk without getting weary or faint. I will trust in You, Lord, forever! Amen!

REFLECTION: What causes you to want to be weary and faint, but you waited on the Lord, mounted up, and ran instead? What did the Lord have you do to renew your strength?

_____

_____

Day 11

Equipped for Service

re you feeling unequipped? Don't think you can handle the tasks before you? Let the Holy Spirit empower you for any task that the Lord assigns you! Just make sure it's a "God-given task" and not a "self-given task." Let God give you the heart of the greatest SERVANT who ever lived — JESUS! Greatness in the kingdom is *servanthood* that begins in the heart! Are you willing to serve others or do you want others to serve you? Privilege always brings with it responsibility! Take the time to pause and calmly think on that!

PRAYER:

Lord, You have not forsaken those who seek You with all their heart. Thank You for taking away the fear of being forsaken. Thank You for being a refuge in times of trouble. Father God, let me always feel an awareness of Your presence! In Jesus' name, I pray. Amen!

REFLECTION: In what new way does God want you to serve, and why? What additional ways do you need to be equipped for service?

_____

_____

_____

_____

_____

_____

_____

_____

_____

_____

_____

_____

_____

_____

_____

_____

_____

_____

_____

_____

_____

_____

_____

_____

Day 12

Commit it to God

> "For this reason, I also suffer these things; nevertheless I am not ashamed, for I know whom I have believed and am persuaded that He is able to keep what I have committed to Him until that Day." -2 Timothy 1:1

Have you committed everything to God? Are you sure that you have? What is stopping you from committing everything to Him, and why? Sometimes we commit partial things into the Lord's hands because we have been persuaded, we can do better. That's a lie from the enemy.

God is able to keep only those things we commit to Him in every area of our life: family, job, church, problems, or circumstances. Whatever it is, believe, and be persuaded to commit it to the Lord.

PRAYER:

Father God, I commit all that I am, that I have, and going through to You! I trust to leave it in Your hands, in Jesus' name, I pray. Amen!

REFLECTION: For every shameful thought the enemy tried to give you recently, seek God on which Scripture you can stand on and commit it to your mind.

_____

_____

_____

_____

_____

_____

_____

_____

_____

_____

_____

_____

_____

_____

_____

_____

_____

_____

_____

_____

_____

_____

_____

_____

_____

Day 13

Touch Me

> "For she said to herself, 'If only I may touch His garment, I shall be made well.' But Jesus turned around, and when He saw her He said, 'Be of good cheer, daughter; your faith has made you well.' And the woman was made well from that hour." -Matthew 9:21-22

Matthew tells the story about a woman, diseased with an issue of blood, who touched the hem of Jesus' garment and was made whole. As God, the Father, He always knew "who" and "where" the woman was. Just like He knows who you are and where you are with your issues in life! Like Jesus, the Teacher, every moment becomes a teaching moment to glorify God! Not only for the disciples, but for us today to develop our faith! No matter how low the issues have brought you in life, you're never too low to reach for Christ! And Jesus Christ is never too far that He can't feel the faith of your touch!

PRAYER:

Father, thank You for making me whole! You see all and comfort me with Your Holy Spirit! May I always feel the touch of Jesus Christ upon my heart, spirit, mind, and body! In Jesus' name, I pray. Amen!

REFLECTION: What new area does God want to develop your faith in? What are you reaching out for Christ to touch in your life?

_____

_____

_____

_____

_____

_____

_____

_____

_____

_____

_____

_____

_____

_____

_____

_____

_____

_____

_____

_____

_____

_____

_____

_____

_____

Day 14

In Time You Will Heal

> "For I am the Lord who heals you."
>
> -Exodus 15:26

I don't know if "time heals all wounds." It doesn't actually heal anything, but I believe that time allows you to get through the wounds! It's God who heals the hurting, wounded heart, and HE will heal and comfort you — if you allow Him!

The hurts, pain, and frustration of the past do not have to dictate your future and cause bitterness to take root! Don't speak what the enemy plants in your thoughts. They can become words that bring discouragement, depression, and a lot of other ugly "d" words. Divine healing results can happen when your thoughts are exchanged with the mind of Christ. Speaking the enemy's word curses over yourself and others should stop when you notice the negative it is manifesting. Apply the thoughts and the words that God plants in your mind, and you will experience victory. Then you can help others in the pits to experience that same victory.

You have the GREATER one within you to help change your life and live it abundantly! All you have to do is change your attitudes and let God change your spiritual altitude! He knows what He is doing! Let God continue to transform and heal your mind and heart!

PRAYER:

Father God, thank You for healing my hurting heart! Thank You for not allowing bitterness to consume me! You are the Lord who heals in whatever afflictions I may encounter. May You continue to transform my mind and heart, in Jesus' name, I pray. Amen!

REFLECTION: What recent hurts kept you from getting the help you needed? What strategies did God give you to release the frustration?

_____

_____

_____

_____

_____

_____

_____

_____

_____

_____

_____

_____

_____

_____

_____

_____

_____

_____

_____

_____

Day 15

Assume the Call

> "But the Lord said to me: "Do not say, 'I am a youth,' For you shall go to all to whom I send you, And whatever I command you, you shall speak. Do not be afraid of their faces, For I am with you to deliver you," says the Lord." -Jeremiah 1:7-8

Never be reluctant to assume your prophetic calling based on your age and ability to speak. Do not despise youths who step into their calling early. You might think you are too old or young, but God doesn't put those limits on you. God can and will do a work in you, just like He did with Jeremiah! Answer the Call! The hardest thing in the world is "to try to do or be something" that God didn't make, equip, ordain, or call you to do or be! This happens when you don't understand what you are, by the will of God. God created you for a purpose! Make your calling and election sure. Know what you are by the will of God and fulfill your God-ordained purpose in Christ!

PRAYER:

Father God, in the name of Jesus, empower me with a stronger anointing to do and walk the paths You have called me to, fearlessly — with all boldness in Your might, power, and Spirit! Amen!

REFLECTION: What is it that you think you are too young or old to do, but God is saying differently? What is really causing you to set limits on yourself?

Day 16

You are Loved

"Yes, I have loved you with an everlasting love; Therefore with lovingkindness I have drawn you." -Jeremiah 31:3

There has never been a day that you have not been loved by your Father! He has always loved you with an everlasting love and always will! All that He has ever done for you has been rooted in that love. That's why He sent Jesus Christ to die in your place, that through Him, you shall live in eternity! You just rest in your Father's love.

PRAYER:

Father God, grant Your children assurance and a strong awareness of the love You have for us! Let us know within every fiber of our being, that You always will be there for us with Your everlasting love! In Jesus' name, I pray. Amen!

REFLECTION: In what ways have you recently witnessed the assurance of God's love for you?

_____

_____

_____

Day 17

Don't Let Betrayal Surprise You

> "I have sinned by betraying innocent blood."
> -Matthew 27:4

here can be an opportunity for betrayal to happen in life, even if we are an innocent party. Sometimes, it can be done by those who are the closest to us. Jesus knew how it felt to go through this type of betrayal. He taught on and illustrated how a person could be betrayed by someone close. When He was celebrating the Passover with His Disciples, He told them in Matthews 26:21 that, "One of you will betray Me." He knowingly chose His betrayer, and Judas sought the opportunity to betray Him.

How many of us, unknowingly, choose our Judas? How many people around, like Judas, seek the opportunity to betray us? Betrayal didn't stop Jesus from fulfilling His purpose! Don't let it stop you from fulfilling yours! 1 Thessalonians 5:15 says, "See that no one renders evil for evil to anyone, but always pursue what is good both for yourselves and for all." It's a hurt that you can get over with forgiveness, prayer, and God's healing that takes place in your heart.

Psalm 55:12-14 reads in the AMP, "For it is not an enemy who reproaches and taunts me—then I might bear it; nor is it one who has hated me who insolently vaunts himself against me—then I might hide from him. But it was you, a man my equal, my companion and my familiar friend. We had sweet fellowship together and used to walk to the house of God in company."

You expect to be hated by your enemies, but you just don't expect your enemies to be the people closest to you. Are you still surprised? Why would you be? Remember, Jesus had his Judas! Also, remember that God has your back! He's more powerful than the enemy, and He has already provided the solution!

PRAYER:

Father God, I never saw the betrayal coming, but since it was allowed to happen, let my heart stay right before You! Never let me betray others. If a cup of betrayal cannot pass away from me unless I drink it, then I'll know it will fulfill kingdom purpose. Your will be done! If it happens, I choose to forgive the offense of betrayal and the offender. In Jesus' name, I pray. Amen!

REFLECTION: In what area of your life have you felt betrayed? If you have encountered betrayal, let God heal your heart. Let Him show you ways to walk out your healing.

_____

_____

_____

_____

_____

_____

_____

_____

_____

_____

Day 18

Finish Your Assignment

"Therefore we also, since we are surrounded by so great a cloud of witnesses, let us lay aside every weight, and the sin which so easily ensnares us, and let us run with endurance the race that is set before us, looking unto Jesus, the author and finisher of our faith, who for the joy that was set before Him endured the cross, despising the shame, and has sat down at the right hand of the throne of God."

-Hebrews 12:1-2

Have you ever had an assignment that you wanted to run from? If we saw all of the persecutions, rejections, deception, and betrayal ahead of time that some of our assignments bring, how many would have taken them on?

An assignment is a position, post, or office which one is assigned. It's a specified task, amount of work assigned, or undertaken assigned by authority. When the assignments are God-given, they do not always mean that you will like or enjoy them, nor does it mean that the people involved will like or enjoy you!

In this race, the Lord has assignments for all of us to complete. Many times, it can put a strain on our endurance. God has used many teachers, family members, friends, and ministries to help prepare and train you to complete your assignments successfully! Do you recognize them? Your labor is not done in vain! You are not alone. God's presence is with you. In this season, God is saying, don't be like Jonah . . . don't flee from the presence of the Lord! It's okay to run, as long as you run into the arms of Jesus! Your cloud of witnesses is cheering you on. He has not left us to run this race alone. Run the race to win souls for Christ.

....

PRAYER:

Father God, thank You for surrounding us with such a great cloud of witnesses! We choose to lay aside every weight and snare, to run this race with endurance and to finish well. Let us always continue to look toward Christ, the author and finisher of our faith. In Jesus' name, I pray. Amen!

....

REFLECTION: Think about a difficult assignment you found hard to fulfill. What made it hard or easy to do?

_____

_____

_____

_____

_____

_____

_____

_____

_____

_____

_____

_____

_____

Determine to Become a Finished Product

"O house of Israel, can I not do with you as this potter?" says the Lord. "Look, as the clay is in the potter's hand, so are you in My hand, O house of Israel!" -Jeremiah 18:6

Do you ever feel like the house of Israel on the potter's wheel? Do you feel that God is tearing you down and remolding you over and over and over again? You cry out to Him, saying, "When will this be over, Lord? What You are doing is killing me! Are you trying to kill me? Why are you allowing this to happen in my life? It is draining my strength! It hurts too much! Are You finished yet?"

Then God takes you in His arms, wipes away your tears, and whispers in your ear, "My child, I'm not finished with you yet, until MY glory can be seen in you! No, this is not designed to kill you, but it is designed to make you better! Everything that I am doing is to make you, now, into My finished product. I have to mold you! I have to make you! I have to shape you! I have to dress you! Yes, my child, I'm even altering and adjusting you to become my finished product! All so you can be an impact in My kingdom!"

Becoming a finished product is always possible when you are used as clay in the Potter's hands. Determine to become His finished product, no matter what's the cost.

PRAYER:

Lord, You are the Potter, I am the clay. Mold me and shape me into a finished product for Your Kingdom's purpose! In Jesus' name, I pray. Amen!

REFLECTION: What circumstances have kept you on the potter's wheel over and over again? How did it make you feel?

_____

_____

_____

_____

_____

_____

_____

_____

_____

_____

_____

_____

_____

_____

_____

_____

_____

_____

Faith on Fire

"That the genuineness of your faith, being much more precious than gold that perishes, though it is tested by fire, may be found to praise, honor, and glory at the revelation of Jesus Christ . . ." -1 Peter 1:7

W*hen the trials of* life seem to test your faith, trust in the Lord. When your faith seems like it is on fire, trust in the Lord. When the trials of life seem to overwhelm you, trust in the Lord. The Lord is saying that these trials will show your faith is genuine. It may be tested, but let your faith remain strong through the trials!

You may be in a storm now! This is not your first storm. Many have been through storms of losses and grief that caused much pain. Don't let the pain control you — let God!

You may feel like you're stuck in an intense state of mourning. You may feel like you are being stabbed in the heart over and over and over again. You may feel like things or people are adding to your sorrow and not towards your healing! God has you, so you don't have to let the pains of life, things, or people, consume or set your faith on fire. They are enemies to our souls! Let God arise and let His enemies of your faith be scattered!

PRAYER:

Lord, thank You, Lord, for genuine faith! Thank You for keeping my faith strong in the midst of the fire. Thank You for allowing the trials to bring praise, glory, and honor as Jesus is revealed to the world. In Jesus' name, I pray. Amen!

. . . .

REFLECTION: What has triggered a complicated grief moment in your life to test your faith and why?

_____

_____

_____

_____

_____

_____

_____

_____

_____

_____

_____

_____

_____

_____

_____

_____

Day 21

When God Says Move

> "Then the LORD said to Moses, "Why are you crying out to me? Tell the Israelites to move on.".-Exodus 14:15 (NIV)

When the Israelites were facing the Red Sea with the Egyptians marching after them, they were terrified and cried out to the Lord. Perhaps they thought they were stuck between two hard places. What do you do when God says "move," and you see no way out? It could be a move that terrified you, to leave a comfort zone. Are you ready to "move" when God tells you to "move and go"? Are you ready to move when He selects the timing? Are you ready to move when He tells you "how, where, and when", without you ever knowing the "why"?

God has people assigned to our hands that He wants us to reach. He has things assigned to our lives that He wants us to complete. Do you have a willingness to be obedient to the things of God, even when you don't understand? Then move past your fears in simple movements of obedience with God. We all need encouragement to move forward in the things of the Lord. God knows who to use to send them!

Even with your move, keep adding, multiplying, and developing in the Kingdom of God. Your move is fulfilling a purpose for change. Let this move push you forward to be a blessing to others.

PRAYER:

Father God, I will trust this move that You are leading me on. I will fulfill Your Will. In Jesus' name, I pray. Amen!

REFLECTION: What area of your life is God telling you to move in? Are you resisting or assisting with the move?

_____

_____

_____

_____

_____

_____

_____

_____

_____

_____

_____

_____

_____

_____

_____

_____

_____

_____

_____

Day 22

Count the Cost

"For which of you, intending to build a tower, does not sit down first and count the cost, whether he has enough to finish . . ."
-Luke 14:28

G od gave us the ministry of reconciliation that, by our example, we might bring others to Him. God can assign us a church or a person to minister with. Stepping out can come with a cost. Don't let the enemy use you to bleed on God's people, due to unhealed hurts. Bleeding will have you attacking people instead of feeding them, and to fulfill your agenda, instead of God's.

If you teach "from" your hurt, you can help others. If you teach "in" your hurt, you end up hurting others!

There's a cost to ministry that a vessel might endure when stepping into what God called you to do. It can include pain, rejections, loss of relationships, trials, seasons of wilderness, and spiritual warfare. But we won't pay what it cost Jesus Christ — His life!

When you leave hindrances to follow Christ, make sure there's enough in you, from God, to count the cost! When we are obedient to what the Lord calls us to do or say, He is always with us! Even when adverse circumstances surround you, see through the eyes of faith in the Lord and His Word!

PRAYER:

Father God, I counted the cost and will continue to build as You lead and direct, Lord. In Jesus' name, I pray. Amen!

REFLECTION: What happened when you stepped out and didn't consider, or count, the cost to build?

_____

_____

_____

_____

_____

_____

_____

_____

_____

_____

_____

_____

_____

_____

_____

_____

_____

_____

_____

_____

_____

Day 23

Let Your Fruit Be Developed

"But the fruit of the Spirit is love, joy, peace, longsuffering, kindness, goodness, faithfulness, gentleness, self-control." -Galatians 5:22-23

As God develops the Fruit of the Spirit within you, don't let challenges or life's painful situations cloud your vision of God's goodness! He is still good, no matter how the enemy tries to use emotions, difficulties, and circumstances to tell you the opposite. God has a higher standard that is developing Christ's character within you! Continue in His process because it's all for your good!

When things in life are hard for you, don't give up on Jesus. You are an elect of God! Don't give up when the going gets tough! You are a conqueror in Christ Jesus! In fact, you're more than a conqueror! You are loved by God! And no power, no matter 'what or who' shall separate you from that love of God! Keep your eyes on the Lord, who already provides the help that you need to be developed.

PRAYER:

Father God, thank You for Your Holy Spirit and for being present with me always. Thank You for the fruit of the Spirit. I thank You for everything You have already done, for everything You are doing, and for everything You are going to do through me. In Jesus' name, I pray. Amen!

REFLECTION: Which aspect of the Fruit of the Spirit is the most challenging for you to walk in? Why?

_____

_____

_____

_____

_____

_____

_____

_____

_____

_____

_____

_____

_____

_____

_____

_____

_____

_____

_____

_____

_____

_____

_____

_____

_____

Get Outside the Box

"Now the Lord is the Spirit; and where the Spirit of the Lord is, there is liberty." -2 Corinthians 3:17

re people trying to box you in to prevent you from experiencing liberty? Refuse to settle for life inside a box that others have placed you in! The Lord desires you to flow in liberty! It's time to rock that boat and be free! Everything has a cutoff time stamp to it! It may be through natural death or through God's shifting of people in and out of your life to fulfill His purpose! He wants you to be a part of the shifting and accomplish your purpose outside the box! A reset is in progress, and His purpose will be fulfilled. It's time to get out of the box that others have put you in!

PRAYER:

Father God, by the power of the Holy Spirit, I declare freedom and empowerment to fulfill Your purpose! In Jesus' name, I pray. Amen!

REFLECTION: How do you react when you can't experience liberty in the areas you know you should be free? Where and why are you not experiencing freedom right now?

_____

_____

_____

_____

_____

_____

_____

_____

_____

_____

_____

_____

_____

_____

_____

_____

_____

_____

_____

_____

_____

_____

Day 25

Comfort in Tough Times

"I, even I, am He who comforts you."
-Isaiah 51:12a

When *tough times come* — because they do come in life — find comfort in the Lord! You might not like wilderness season, but realize much is happening during those times. Even when you can't see, hear, sense, or feel Him, trust what you believe and know about Him. His presence is right there with you, and He will never forsake you. It is well because the joy of the Lord is your strength! Your praise is your weapon! Never allow your present situation, no matter how dark it may be, steal your worship for God!

Sometimes those tough times make us fearful. 2 Timothy 1:7 reads, "For God has not given us a spirit of fear, but of power and of love and of a sound mind." It didn't say we will never experience fear! When we feel it, we know from His Word that He didn't give it to us! Turn from fear and send it back to the enemy because you don't need it! God has given you the ability to walk in the power of the Lord!

PRAYER:

Father God, thank You, Lord, that You have not given me a spirit of fear! Thank You for giving the greatest Comforter within me! In Jesus' name, I pray. Amen!

REFLECTION: In what ways, situations, or places have you experienced the Comforter? How has He used you to comfort others?

_____

_____

_____

_____

_____

_____

_____

_____

_____

_____

_____

_____

_____

_____

_____

_____

_____

_____

_____

_____

_____

_____

_____

_____

Day 26

Changed Plans

> "For I know the thoughts that I think toward you, says the Lord,
> thoughts of peace and not of evil, to give you a future and a hope."
> -Jeremiah 29:11

Life sometimes brings change that we might not understand. People may no longer be around that we thought would be here. It may have been by death, divorce, strained relationships, or church membership changes. We may not be in the places or positions we thought we would be in. And then, here comes another blockage or change from the Lord. It may leave you wondering, "What in the world is going on, Lord!" When God blocks, His way is always better, because He has the plans! Our purposes, goals, and plans may shift when we line up with God's will. The Lord is telling you, "You asked me to lead you. I'm in control of the situation! Just follow My plans. . . even when it changes your plans!"

PRAYER:

Father God, there are still plans and purposes You have for me to fulfill. Let me not abandon those things that will put me on the paths of destiny. Lead me, Lord. In Jesus' name, I pray. Amen!

REFLECTION: What personal plans did you think you were going to fulfill, but the Lord just switched your focus for His purpose to be fulfilled instead?

_____

_____

_____

_____

_____

_____

_____

_____

_____

_____

_____

_____

_____

_____

_____

_____

_____

_____

_____

_____

_____

_____

Day 27

Nothing is Common about You

> "For 'who has known the mind of the Lord that he may instruct Him?'
> But we have the mind of Christ." -1 Corinthians 2:16

As believers, *we must* have the mind of the Lord in ALL things! Not in some things, small things, or big things only, but in ALL things! Don't allow someone to belittle you into what they think! Don't let them make you feel inferior by their remarks to use your "common" sense.

Common can mean many things. It can mean a lack of privilege or special status. It can also mean falling below ordinary standards or being second-rate. It can mean you're not in any way special, strange, or unusual. It can suggest inferiority when the person is looking down on you because they think they're the superior one.

Why would you want second-rate senses guiding your decisions? We are told from the Word of God to "Trust in the Lord with all your heart, And lean not on your own understanding; In all your ways acknowledge Him, And He shall direct your paths." Don't settle for the "common sense" when you have the mind of Christ available to direct you!

Father God, I trust You to direct my paths, with all my heart! My Lord and Savior, instruct me in ALL my doing. I will not lean on my own understanding, or on something "common" to lead me on a path that You have not directed or chosen for me! In Jesus' name, I pray. Amen!

REFLECTION: Think of those who have tried to belittle you with their words and forgive them. Now ask God about the word curses that may have been released; turn them into blessings instead.

_____

_____

_____

_____

_____

_____

_____

_____

_____

_____

_____

_____

_____

_____

_____

_____

_____

Day 28

Expressions from the Heart

"You are the salt of the earth; but if the salt loses its flavor, how shall it be seasoned? It is then good for nothing but to be thrown out and trampled underfoot by men. You are the light of the world. A city that is set on a hill cannot be hidden." -Matthew 5:13-14

Sometimes, *what's expressed on* social media by Christians is no different from what's expressed by the unsaved. Some Christians out there are cutting and destroying each other with hurtful words, destroying peoples' characters, ministries, or callings.

We are the salt of the earth and the light of the world. We cannot afford to let the enemies cause us to stoop to their level, losing our effectiveness or standards in Christ. You are not my enemy, and I am not yours. If you offend someone in action or word, say you're sorry and ask for forgiveness. Let your heart always be in right standing before the Lord, before the people God assign to you; then you can be an influence for HIS kingdom!

We all have people assigned to our hands that God wants us to reach. They see, along with God, all of the junk that has been placed on the media by Christians that do not reflect Christ in us! Maybe we were not the child, sibling, relative, spouse, in-law, friend, employee, or church member that others thought we should be. All that matters is that we get it right with God and be the person that He has called us to be! If people are going to be bold enough to stand up for the enemy, you should be bold enough to stand for Christ! If you are confessing

Christianity, let it show in everything you do, even on social media, so that God can get the glory!

PRAYER:

Father God, may I never lose my effectiveness as the salt of the earth. May my light always shine in the world to win others for Your kingdom. In Jesus' name, I pray. Amen!

REFLECTION: What have you lost your effectiveness in as the salt of the earth and the light of the world?

_____

_____

_____

_____

_____

_____

_____

_____

_____

_____

_____

_____

_____

_____

_____

Day 29

Love Words of Encouragement

> "For He chose us in Him before the creation of the world to be holy and blameless in His sight." -Ephesians 1:4 NIV

If you're truly in Christ, you are loved, accepted, forgiven, and valued by God. God's people are valuable to Him. Everything that He created has value. Live like someone valued and loved by God! You were the focus of His love, mentioned in the above Scripture. Jeremiah 31:3 reads, "Yes, I have loved you with an everlasting love; Therefore with lovingkindness I have drawn you."

Thank God for keeping you through any crisis or other difficult circumstances in your life. You were built for such a time as this, and God will continue to get the glory! It's a great day to be in the Lord and for you to rejoice! This is a day you've never lived in before. Has the Lord given you dreams and visions yet to be fulfilled? It's not too late to discover and pursue what He has placed in your heart!

He hasn't forsaken you. He's waiting on you! He's saying, "I'm here and always have been. I will never leave you or forsake you. You're MY child, and I love you with an everlasting love. Just trust ME and watch ME work on your behalf!"

PRAYER:

Father God, thank You for choosing me before the foundation of the world. Thank You for loving me with an everlasting love. Thank You for never forsaking me. May I complete and fulfill the assignments, callings, and destinies You have chosen for me. In Jesus' name, I pray. Amen!

REFLECTION: No matter what we are going through, someone else may be going through a rougher time. Search for those within your sphere that you can encourage with the love of God. Your kindness can trigger a response of hope for others to enjoy.

_____

_____

_____

_____

_____

_____

_____

_____

_____

_____

_____

_____

_____

_____

Day 30

Assignment too Hard

> "Show me Your ways, O Lord; Teach me Your paths. Lead me in Your truth and teach me, For You are the God of my salvation; On You I wait all the day." -Psalm 25:4-5

Have you ever angered God because He told you to do something, but you told Him to send someone else to do it because you didn't want, or like, the assignment given? Even in school, we had assignments we did not like, but we did them anyway. Just like Moses, God will be your mouth and teach you what you shall do. You just have to go when and where He tells you to complete the assignments He gives! Don't miss the assignments that can bring greater purpose to your life. Whatever God says to do, just do it! What crucial decision are you about to make, and you need God to show you the way? If He is leading you, you are choosing the right and best path! Trust His leading and begin to align with His will! Decide to submit and stay in His will for clear directions.

PRAYER:

Father God, show me Your ways and paths to walk in. May Your truth always lead me. In Jesus' name, I pray. Amen!

REFLECTION: No assignment God gives is too hard with Him. What is He now telling you to do that you have not done yet?

_____

_____

_____

_____

_____

_____

_____

_____

_____

_____

_____

_____

_____

_____

_____

_____

_____

_____

_____

_____

_____

_____

_____

_____

_____

_____

_____

_____

_____

DECLARING BLESSINGS TO MY FUTURE GENERATIONS

> "One generation shall praise Your works to another, And shall declare Your mighty acts." -Psalm 145:4

L*ife can take us* through circumstances we might like to bypass. If we did bypass some, we might have missed some valuable information learned in the wilderness seasons. When I wrote this book, I thought about my grandchildren. My thoughts were, "What could I leave as an inheritance, in writing, for my future generations? How could I bless them? What would I want them to know if I was not around? How could they learn not to repeat the same mistakes that previous generations made before them if no one tells them?"

God spoke to my spirit and said, "Leave them a book. Give them nuggets of words of wisdom that you used to keep your heart right through life's circumstances. Therefore, if they ever want to know what a previous generation did, show them that you prayed and declared MY MIGHTY ACTS in your life! Leave blessings to help point them to My Word, no matter what they're encountering in life!"

The stories, instructions, daily devotions, or blessings we leave our future generations can be helpful and important to them later in life, especially when we are no longer around. We can leave an inheritance to bless future seeds for many years to come. When we have given them God's Word of Life, we've given them the best gift to bring them through the many situations of life. This is an inheritance for my future generation! I leave you sweet inspirations and declarations from the Lord when times are tough, or when you want to know what your previous generation did when they encountered similar times.

For times when the enemy tries to bring you into bondage situations: I declare you will break away and flow with the Spirit of liberty in every atmosphere! (See: 2 Corinthians 3:17)

When you don't understand things in life: I declare a greater awareness of God's wisdom, knowledge and understanding to be release in you! (See: Proverbs 2:6, 9:10; Isaiah 11:2)

When you have trouble speaking truth: I declare that you always speak the truth in love as you grow up in all things in Christ! (See: Ephesians 4:15)

When you have anything against anyone: I declare the Spirit of forgiveness will overtake you! (See: Mark 11:24-26)

When life, challenges, and things seem hard: I declare you will experience a strong reliance and belief on the Lord, for nothing is too hard for Him! (See: Genesis 18:14; Jeremiah 32:17, 27)

When you let go of peace due to troublesome situations: I declare you shall regain your peace and will not let your heart be troubled nor afraid! (See: Mark 4:39; John 14:27)

When you are besieged by the enemy power: I declare you shall take it back and walk in the authority Christ has given you! (See: Luke 10:19)

When fear tries to come upon you: I declare you are fearless with God's power, love, and a sound mind! (See: 2 Timothy 1:7)

When people are not there for you: I declare God always will be, never to forsake you! (See: Deuteronomy 31:6, 8; Joshua 1:5; Hebrews 13:5)

In trouble, when you cannot call on anyone: I declare you will call on your Deliverer and honor and glorify Him with your praise! (See: Psalm 50:15)

When you feel weak: I declare you are strong, strengthened, and empowered in the grace of Christ Jesus! (See: 2 Timothy 2:1)

When fretting about growth where you are: I declare you shall be blessed and your territory enlarged! (See: 1 Chronicles 4:10)

When you are seeking a plan for your life: I declare that you shall know God's plans for your life, and they will prosper and give you hope! (See: Jeremiah 29:11)

When you need direction: I declare your steps shall be established, made firm, directed, secured, and ordered by the Lord! (See: Psalm 37:23)

When facing difficulties: I declare you shall be strengthened and hardened to difficulties because God will hold you up! (See: Isaiah 41:10)

When your esteem is affected: I declare you shall find favor and high esteem with God and man! (See: Proverb 3:4; Luke 2:52)

When you don't know what to seek: I declare you shall seek first the kingdom of God to rule over you, and His righteousness will transform your life! (See: Matthew 6:33)

When you don't feel love: I declare you shall have a great awareness of God's steadfast, covenant, loyalty, and everlasting love and be drawn by His loving-kindness! (See: Jeremiah 31:3)

When you need strength: I declare you will do God-ordained things through Christ, who will strengthen you! (See: Philippians 4:13)

When you need to follow truth: I declare the Spirit of truth shall guide and lead you! (See: John 14:17, 15:26, 16:13)

When overtaken by trials: I declare you will experience God's joy through any trials, tests, or temptations! (See: John 16:13, 33; James 1:2-3)

When you need healing: I declare God's Word will heal and deliver you! (See: Psalm 107:20)

When you need courage: I declare you shall be of good courage, and your heart strengthened! (See: Psalm 27:14, 31:24)

When you draw away from God: I declare you shall resist the devil and you shall draw near to God! (See: James 4:7-8)

When cares lead you to worry: I declare that you will cast all your cares upon God, for He cares for you! (See: 1 Peter 5:7)

When it is hard for you to trust: I declare your trust shall remain in the Lord and you will feed on His faithfulness! (See: Psalm 37:3)

When you feel restless: I declare you shall be still and know God! (See: Psalm 46:10)

When you want to display God's fruit: I declare you will have love, joy, peace, longsuffering, kindness, goodness, faithfulness, gentleness, and self-control release within you to show the Fruit of the Spirit. (See: Galatians 5:22-23)

When you're wondering about your gifts: I declare you will show unity in the diversity of your spiritual gifts! (See: 1 Corinthians 12)

When in prayer: I declare your prayer will never cease, but will be effective and fervent as a righteous child of God! (See: James 5:16; 1 Thessalonians 5:17)

BE BLESSED FUTURE GENERATIONS

I pray you always choose to walk in forgiveness, even when it is very hard to do. Always hold fast to the profession of your faith, without wavering, because God is faithful! May you always walk by faith and not by sight!

I pray you live a God-ordained life, fulfilling His purposes and plans for you! Whatever God teaches you, I pray that you continue to pass down those teachings to your future generations.

I pray that you will not become weary in doing good, for at the proper time, you will reap a harvest, if you do not give up!

May the Holy Spirit's presence always be felt, sensed, and trusted in your life. May God reveal and destroy every trap, snare, trick, plan, and problem from the enemy! May every curse be turned, instead, into a blessing!

For those married, I pray that your marriages will be a representative of Christ's love for the church! For every married male, I pray your wife will see the love of you, submitting to the Lord as you lead her with a servant's heart! For every married female, I pray you will be able to trust the leading of a God-fearing man, and that you both will be able to submit one to another, out of reverence to Christ!

May God build a hedge of protection around all He has entrusted to you, and that your home stays fully cleansed, spiritually! May your home be built with God's wisdom, understanding, and knowledge!

I seal this prayer in the blood and mighty name of Jesus.

AMEN!

Appendix II

Warring Marriage Prayers

> "Confess your trespasses to one another, and pray for one another, that you may be healed. The effective, fervent prayer of a righteous man avails much." -James 5:16

Not *every marriage has* a "happily ever after" story without any problems. Some may experience times of turmoil that only the Lord can bring them through to a place of happiness. Many marriages have been affected by deceit, lies, infidelity, and unfaithfulness.

Although I know it can happen to any male or female, there are many Leah's and Hosea's who have suffered the effects of a bad marriage. Some may have been rejected, replaced, unwanted, and definitely unloved, like Leah. Some may have been married to a person who proved to be unfaithful, but they were called to walk in faithfulness, like Hosea's marriage to Gomer.

No one ever expects to give love and trust and then have that trust betrayed by a faithless spouse. God knows the feeling because many of His people have been unfaithful to Him. If the Lord can restore our relationship when we have been unfaithful to Him, surely He can restore those marriages when both parties have repentant hearts. It's time to war on behalf of our God-ordain marriages!

Father God, in the name of Jesus, thank You for allowing me to enter into Your presence! You are an awesome God and judge.

I petition You to allow my prayer request to come before Your court. Lord, I ask You to be the judge between my marriage and Satan.

I declare that I am in covenant with You, Jesus, and the Holy Spirit! Just like You are the God of Abraham, Isaac, and Jacob, You are my God! You're my Heavenly Father, Jesus is my Savior, and the Holy Spirit lives within me!

I seek an emergency DIVINE INTERVENTION, issued by Your court of heaven, to PROTECT the destiny of our marriage that You have for us to fulfill! You are our ENFORCER, FATHER GOD!

Father God, You are our defender and protector! You are our ultimate defense and our place of refuge! You are our merciful and gracious God!

You are our banner of love! You are victorious over all, including our lives! You have been victorious throughout the generations to all who call on You in faith!

We call on You with much expectation, to see and experience victory in our marriage, because You are our hiding place and I put all of my trust in You!

Jesus said, "It is finished," on the cross! I believe and declare the enemy attacks are also finished, so we can have victory in our marriage!

AGREE WITH THE WORD OF GOD

Scripture tells us in Matthew 18:18 (AMPC) - "Whatever you forbid and declare to be improper and unlawful on earth, must be what is already forbidden in heaven, and whatever you permit and declare proper and lawful on earth, must be what is already permitted in heaven."

Father God, in the name of Jesus, I lift up our marriage and these prayer petitions before You! Thank You, Lord, for always answering prayers prayed according to YOUR will and YOUR Word, and I am totally in agreement with them.

It is written in MATTHEW 19:5-6 ". . . and said, 'For this reason a man will leave his father and mother and be united to his wife, and the two will become one flesh?' So they are no longer two, but one flesh. Therefore what God has joined together, let no one separate."

May we always pray effectively over each other, our relationship, distressing situations, our marriage, and our family, so our prayers can always avail much!

Father God, I believe that no weapon formed against us shall prosper and every tongue, which rises against us in judgment, we do condemn. This is our heritage as a servant of the Lord, and our righteousness is from You.

Father God, in the name of Jesus, Your righteous hand is with us, to bind us closer together. It is written in Isaiah 41:10 - "Fear not, for I am with you; Be not dismayed, for I am your God. I will strengthen you, Yes, I will help you, I will uphold you with My righteous right hand." Strengthen and uphold us, Lord. In Jesus' name!

Though we walk in the midst of trouble, You will revive us! You will stretch out Your hand against the wrath of our enemies, and Your right hand will save us.

Father God, it is written in Malachi 2:16, "For the Lord God of Israel says "That He hates divorce, For it covers one's garment with violence . . ."

Lord, let us not cover our marriage garment with violence. It's not Your will for God-ordained marriages to fail, because You hate divorce! Therefore, in the name of Jesus, let not our marriage fail!

WALK IN FORGIVENESS

Father God, in the name of Jesus: Thank You for creating a clean heart and renewing a steadfast right spirit within us! Search out our hearts and empower us, Lord, to keep forgiving each other always in obedience to Your will!

Where we're not totally free from sin, we need Your forgiveness for our individual wrongdoings! We ask You to forgive every sin we have committed, omitted, spoken out of ignorance, done to one another, or to others!

Don't let anger drive us apart, but instead, let forgiveness draw us together toward You!

We trust Your Word! We believe Your promise that righteousness will produce peace and a quiet life within us! We desire peace within our marriage and life, Lord!

Your Word tells us to love our enemies and to pray and bless those who persecute us.

We forgive those who may have wronged us in any way or caused problems within our relationship.

Therefore, Lord, for those who speak, pray or come against us, or our marriage seeking harm, I choose to forgive them, and I bless them in the name of Jesus.

THE BLOOD OF JESUS CHRIST

Father, I proclaim that I am covered under the blood of Jesus as Your child! By faith, I have been made righteous because I am in right standing with You!

Let every path of witchcraft or evilness that has entered into our lives be overturned by the BLOOD of JESUS!

The enemy has no legal right to use weapons to steal, kill, and destroy my marriage. As a believer in Christ, I have not given the enemy that right, nor have You! I am a blood-bought child of God — bought with the blood of Jesus Christ!

"For though we walk in the flesh, we do not war according to the flesh. For the weapons of our warfare are not carnal, but mighty in God, for pulling down strongholds . . ." -2 Corinthians 10:3-4

"We wrestle not against flesh and blood, but against principalities, against powers, against the rulers of the darkness of this age . . ." and against spiritual hosts of wickedness in the heavenly places. I pray for deliverance from the enemies using us or others to attack and destroy our marriage!

Father God, in the name of Jesus, I renounce, cancel and rebuke all word curses, hexes, vexes, spells, incantations, and every expression of witchcraft spoken over our lives or marriage, and declare they shall, instead, be turned into blessings!

Lord, every manipulative spirit, ungodly soul ties, ungodly boundaries, and witchcraft spirits, from others against us, I cancel their assignment, power and destroy them from the roots in the name of Jesus!

Father God, because we are to cast "down imagination, and every high thing that exalts itself against the knowledge of God, and brings into captivity every thought to the obedience of Christ", in the name of Jesus:

I cast down and remove every scheme of the enemy, causing wrong thoughts to enter into our minds and build walls of lies! I make a declaration to no longer give up control of my mind to the enemy's thoughts! My mind is subject to the obedience of Christ!

Father God, in the name of Jesus: Whatever "Hindrances, strongholds, spirits" the enemy used to plant seeds of discord, deception, divisions, confusion, strife, plots, traps, or snares into our hearts or relationship, destroy and remove these powers from the very root of our midst and marriage!

Lord, You gave us authority to trample on serpents and scorpions, and over all of the power of the enemy, and nothing shall by any means hurt us.

We forbid demonic interferences with the work of the Holy Spirit, in how He uses us to pray. Therefore, we use our authority to snatch our marriage out of the hands of the kingdom of darkness, back into the kingdom of God, and claim that now in Jesus' name!

In the name of Jesus, I place our marriage under Your divine authority and protection. Thank You for fighting for us now, in the spiritual realm! I believe You are moving heaven and earth to save us from the temptations and schemes of destruction at work, from the enemy, in our marriage now!

The enemy of our soul is no match for You, Lord! He is not all-knowing, he is not all-powerful, and he is not ever-present, but You are! He is not Lord over the heavens, the earth, and the things under the earth, but You are! He is a wicked one that runs when no one is chasing him! He cannot run to You and be safe, but we can and we will!

In the name of Jesus, prevent us from fighting each other, but instead, to fight our enemies in the spirit and battles in prayer!

Thank You, Lord, for removing the power of those who try to influence us in a negative way! I command them to free their hold upon our lives and marriage, in Jesus' name!

Let God arise, and His enemies be scattered! Arise, Lord, and bring shame on every power that tries to challenge our marriage!

As You rise up, Lord, let us do the same for our marriage to work according to Your plan! As You rise up within us, let us rise up against the evil at work in our marriage! Lord, we know You will cause our enemies who rise up against us to be defeated before us, in Jesus' name!

Bind the strongman working against us in our hearts, and release the SPIRIT of TRUTH into the atmosphere, allowing clarity to flow instead in our hearts, in Jesus' name!

Let every marriage problem among us BREAK and CEASE! Bind them, Lord, making them unable to attach to us ever again! Release Your heavenly host of warrior angels around us, in the name of Jesus!

When life is very overwhelming between us, I trust You to show us how to resolve all differences! Lord, You are sovereign, not only in the good times, but also in adversities, afflictions, and hardships!

I choose to trust in Your faithfulness during those times! You ordained this marriage, Lord, and we will continue to always seek You faithfully!

GENESIS 12:3 says, "I will bless those who bless you, And I will curse him who curses you; And in you all the families of the earth shall be blessed."

Father God, in the name of Jesus:

The promise to Abraham is a promise for us! Our marriage is BLESSED and ORDAINED by You and is not cursed! Therefore, I plead the blood of Jesus AGAINST the power of the enemy coming between our marriage by words or actions:

Our marriage WILL not be controlled by any demonic forces, in the name of Jesus! I cancel the results and activity of every negative detail fed to us, in the name of Jesus!

Whatever evil agreed upon to chase us away from our home or each other, I cancel the enemy assignments and void them out, in the name of Jesus!

Father God, dissolve and release us from all lies and accusations of the evil ones, in the name of Jesus! I cancel any evil prophecy and negative words spoken concerning us and our marriage, in the name of Jesus!

Let nothing negative happen in our relationship to destroy it due to the plots and plans of the enemy! Let us not be persuaded away from Your plans or purposes for us!

Every plot and plan of those assigned to destroy our home, against us, or our marriage; I cancel your assignment in the name of Jesus!

HEALING AND DELIVERANCE

Father God, in the name of Jesus:

It is written that Jesus came to heal the broken-hearted! Your Word tells us that You are "near to those who have a broken heart." Therefore, You are near us right now, even delivering us in our brokenness!

LORD, because You are Jehovah Rapha, there is a set time for healing to take place, and You are healing our relationship now!

We know there's nothing too hard for You, Lord, even when bad things happen in our relationship! Help us not to focus on disappointing circumstances or situations!

Remove all frustrations, disappointments, and anger that exist between us, so we will not sin against You! Give us deliverance and strength during difficult times, in the grace that is in Christ Jesus!

Take away every pain among us in our marriage! Protect our hearts, minds, and emotions from every attack of the enemy! Align our heart, mind, and will to reflect Yours!

Never ever let our hearts become hardened toward each other! Never, Lord, let our plans or desires blind us to YOUR will for our life as a Christian couple.

We ask You, Lord, to show us how to revive our love the WAY You designed us to love! Lord, may we always turn toward You for guidance to remove ALL the hurts and offenses toward one another.

In the Name of Jesus, tear down the walls of miscommunication between us that have been erected by the enemy! Deliver and save us, Lord!

Lord, when we have obstacles in our marriage, let us come together in unity with You! Help us to follow Your will by restoring and seeking peace between us!

Let not life break us down, but allow us to breakthrough with You in our marriage! Instead of allowing the enemy to push us away from each other, show us how to push the enemy away from this marriage! Let us not be a voice the enemy uses against each other! We refuse to allow ourselves to be deceived by the enemy! In the Name of Jesus, cancel all ridicule, slander, and lies projected against each other before it ever reaches our hearts, minds, and lips! You're greater than the enemy, LORD, and in Christ, we are too!

Father, Your Word says in Psalm 91:15, "He shall call upon Me, and I will answer him; I will be with him in trouble; I will deliver him and honor him."

I call upon You, Lord, with my heart, seeking divine answers and solutions for existing problems in this marriage. I cry out to you, Lord, and make a declaration to stand in the gap. We will not be each other's enemy! I am the spouse and a child of God — called to be by my mate's side!

Father God, in the name of Jesus, as I pour out my heart to You, I will trust You! I will remain faithful, available, and teachable to You!

Father God, Your plans and thoughts are not of evil, but to give us peace, to prosper us and to give us hope! Let no evil thoughts be produced from out of our hearts to stop your plan! Cover our hearts and thought life with the blood of Jesus!

Lord, lead us to the throne of grace, always in prayer, that we may obtain mercy and find grace for help in our time of need!

Whenever we miss the mark with You and each other, remind us that You are always behind the scenes, working on our behalf!

Where fear and anxiety are within us, in the name of Jesus, provide us with a heart change, removing them!

Let us experience a good, Godly, happy, prosperous, successful, and working marriage! Give us a marriage to fulfill Your kingdom call upon our lives, so Your glory will be seen and manifested in our marriage, in Jesus' name we pray!

Remove all unbelief within us! Remind us of Your mercy and loving-kindness, day and night.

Develop us, Lord, into the man and woman of God that You ordained and called us to be!

You offered Jesus as a perfect blood sacrifice so that we both can receive Your undeserved favor! Neither of us deserves Your help, but by grace, we seek Your help right now!

While we wait for answered prayers, we will sing praises of Your might and strength! We choose to wait on You, Lord! We believe Your promises!

We love You, Lord! Thank You for being our River of Life, our portion, and the source of all we need! My heart cries out, declaring that Jesus is Lord over me, my spouse, and our marriage!

DECREES AND DECLARATIONS:

In the name of Jesus:

I decree and declare, we will dwell in the house of the Lord forever! I decree and declare, the glory of our latter home will be GREATER than the former!

I decree and declare, the works of the Lord in our marriage will manifest the GLORY OF GOD!

I decree and declare, the Lord's blessings will continue to chase us down and take us over!

I decree and declare, God's goodness and mercy shall continue to be with us, within us and shall follow us all the days of our lives!

I decree and declare, our marriage WILL LIVE and not die!

I decree and declare, we will continue to cherish and honor each other!

I decree and declare, we will run to you for the right solution and way to respond to each other, according to Christ!

I decree and declare, we will not speak cruel and dishonest remarks toward each other, but we will speak to one another in love!

I decree and declare, we will always care for one another! We will reverse wrong actions from the enemy, in the name of Jesus!

I decree and declare, we will listen to Your instructions, guidance, and walk in forgiveness!

I decree and declare, I will love my spouse, and my spouse will always love me, just like Jesus Christ loved the church, and willingly gave His life for us!

I decree and declare, we will continue to be good trees that cannot bear evil fruit because our roots and fruit are HOLY!

I decree and declare, there will be no retaliation against us from the enemy, neither in any way against our family, jobs, homes, finances, and all that pertain to us!

Thank You, God, for victory in our marriage!
I ask that You answer and seal these *prayer strategies, decrees,*
and *declarations,* all in the precious name of Jesus I pray.

Amen!

www.ingramcontent.com/pod-product-compliance
Lightning Source LLC
LaVergne TN
LVHW051232080426
835513LV00016B/1551